Tzidkus Stands Forever

The Life and Lessons of

Rabbi Menachem Mendel Perr zt"l

Yechiel Yitzchok Perr

COPYRIGHT © 2011

Version 3.5

ALL RIGHTS RESERVED

Contact: chedviperr@gmail.com

FOREWORD – Rabbi Yeshiah Feinroth

"וְאֶת-דּוֹרוֹ מִי יְשׂוֹחֵחַ" (ישעיה נ"ג:ח')

In our current generation, only those who knew the old America can have any sense of the unique contributions of my Rebbe Muvhak, Rav Perr ztvk"l, and of his *mesirus* to each and every individual, no matter how far removed from Judaism. Only they can appreciate his Shlichus el Hador and his success in influencing those who became Bnei Torah and those who remained true Torah Jews. Those who did not experience that world in America's Sohu V'vohu, devoid of Torah and of any feelings of Jewishness, cannot relate to what is described here.

We, who lived with him and were zoche to his influence, can have *some* understanding of what he was, what he did, and how great his accomplishments were. Of course, most of us in that category owe our lives to him. If this book was meant for us and not for the larger community, I am sure it will be appreciated. But beyond our own small circle, people will not be able to fathom his greatness.

Exceptions, of course, are the Gedolei Hador who by virtue of their Gadlus can see beyond their protected universe. I quote two of them. Rav Yisroel Gustman ztvk"l, upon hearing from me that Rav Perr had left this world, said,

"Der velt hot farloren der Tzadik Hador- the world has lost the Tzadik of the generation"

Rav Henoch Leibowitz, ztvk"l, told me that Rav Perr once went to Lakewood to be *mekabel ponim* Rav Aharon ztvk"l. Rav Aharon stood up for him *m'lo komoso*. Rav Perr never came again to Lakewood!

Yeshiah Feinroth

15 Teves 5771

More than what I have read before you

is written here

-Yoma 68b

Tzidkus Stands Forever

A son is both the best and the worst biographer of his father. He is the best biographer, because as a child, he is the best judge of what is an authentic account of his father. But he is also the worst, because he does not have the distance to see his father as a person. To him, his father will always be seen from the acute angle of the small child looking up.

My father never spoke about himself. He was modest and self-effacing, perhaps even shy. However, there were times when a tantalizing bit of personal information would slip out, especially when he wished to teach a lesson, and then I was able to learn many things about him.

As an example: My father was a great masmid. He was always busy doing something important, or else he was learning. And he was always encouraging me to be a masmid as well.

Once, when speaking about hasmodo, he told me that when his own father returned to Drohichin, after having been away a long time in America, he went to speak to my father's rebbe to find out how my father was doing. The rebbe said to him, "Someday he will be the Brisker Rov." Brisk is about a hundred kilometers from Drohichin. Predicting that he would be the Rov of Brisk meant that he would occupy a position much respected in Drohichin; indeed, in all of Lita.

Tzidkus Stands Forever

This prediction about my father's future filled my grandfather with joy, and he repeated it to his own father, who was known in Drohichin as Mordechai Zhaluzher. Zeida Mordechai listened, and then he said to my grandfather, "If you want to know whether this is true, stand at night next to his bed while he sleeps. If he calls out in his sleep, 'Abaya, Rava,' then it's true. If not, then it will never be."

"Nu, Yechiel," my father said to me, "did I become the Brisker Rov?"

From this one little conversation, I understood what a bright youngster and good student my father had been. I also learned how much love and respect for Torah greatness his father and grandfather possessed. And the penetrating insight of my father's grandfather impressed me very much. Yet my father told this to me for none of these reasons; he had intended only to illustrate the importance of hasmodo, based on his own experience.

All his life, my father was indeed a great masmid. As long as I lived at home, I fell asleep every night to the sound of my father's voice learning. And yet, he was never satisfied with himself. He always demanded still more. Nor was my father ever satisfied with his level of avodas Hashem. This was one source of his profound anava.

Sometime after my father passed away, I was talking about him with Rav Yaakov Kamenetsky, when he suddenly

Tzidkus Stands Forever

asked me "Tell me, do you think that your father knew who he was?"

This question had never occurred to me before, and I was silent as I thought it over. But then, as I started to answer, Reb Yaakov interrupted me.

I had been about to respond that my father was indeed aware of his own stature. I had just remembered that once I had seen him make a phone call in which he tried to enlist a prominent Rov in doing a certain mitzvah, and the Rov had refused. My father hung up the phone and muttered to himself, "If he will sit in Gan Eden, I don't want to sit next to him!"

As I started answering Reb Yaakov he interrupted me and said, "But of course he knew who he was! He could never have been the tzadik he became, if he didn't know who he was!"

Rav Yaakov was silent for a moment and then he added, "Such hiddenness! He was almost not a person of this generation at all!"

But it was not only his anava that made my father so self-effacing. My father believed in self-effacement as a midah tovah, and he admired others for possessing it.

There was a Tokayer family in Far Rockaway whose four sons learned in the yeshiva. One day, my father said to me, "You should tell the Tokayer boys that their great-

Tzidkus Stands Forever

grandfather, their mother's grandfather, was a great tzadik." The great grandfather had been known as Michel dem einbinder, which probably means that he was a bookbinder. My father had known him from Drohichin. "Dad," I said to him, "tell me, in what way was he a tzadik?"

"What is there to tell?" my father said with a shrug, "he was a tzadik."

"But these are American kids," I persisted. "If I don't describe him in some way, they just won't understand." "Well then," my father said, "just tell them that he was a quiet man."

A quiet man was the description of a tzadik in my father's understanding. This understanding is, of course, derived from the Gemara in Sanhedrin 88b: "Who is a child of the World to Come? A person who is modest and self-effacing, who enters quietly and leaves quietly, who learns Torah constantly, and who doesn't think he deserves credit for what he does." This Gemara is a good description of my father.

Tzidkus Stands Forever

My grandfather, Yechiel Yitzchok Perr, was born in 1868 to his father, Mordechai Perkovitzky, and his mother, Henya Appelbaum. Zeida Mordechai was sixteen years old when he married, and his first child, Yechiel Yitzchok, was born a year later, so there was only a seventeen-year age difference between father and son. Because of this closeness in age, their relationship was more like that of brothers, rather than that of father and son. My father said that in a way, they even looked like brothers.

Henya Appelbaum was twenty-two at the time of her marriage. She was a poor orphan who had been raised by relatives. At twenty-two, she was already considered an "older girl" in those days, and she had no dowry. Zeida Mordechai married her because she was a great meyucheses from a family of important rabbonim. My father remembered that she was a sheini b'sheini – a first cousin – of the wife of Reb Nochumke Kobriner, the Bialistoker Rebbe.

Bobeh Henya was a very good person, a very smart person, and a tzadekes. She was also very handy. She was able to wire together broken cooking pots. People brought her their broken pots to repair from all over the town. She would charge two kopeks for the repair.

He was not a Rov, but Zeide Mordechai possessed a profound love and respect for talmidei chachamim and Torah learning. There was a machlokes that broke out in Drohichin against the Rov. "Our family stood with the Rov," my father told me.

Tzidkus Stands Forever

Zeide Mordechai's father was called Leibke, and his mother was Chana Malka. Reb Leib was blind, and he used to teach mishnayos to others. He knew shas mishnayos by heart. According to my father, his Hebrew name was probably Yehuda Leib. If so, it's probable that my father's cousin Yehuda Leib Rosenbaum was named after him.

Zeida Mordechai, for at least a substantial part of his life, made his living as a "viner," a winemaker. It is interesting that my father also made wine a few times, using a large earthenware crock in our cellar for this purpose. No doubt this came from what he has seen in his youth. And there is no doubt that Zeida Mordechai who lived together with his daughter-in-law and grandchildren had a profound influence on the family. My father would not put his hat on a table. This was a minhag that many observed, but my father told me that he learned this from his grandfather, who explained that a table is treated with respect because it is used for mitzvos, for eating, and for learning.

Bobeh Henya would make grape jelly from the sediments of her husband's wine, and she would bring containers of her jelly as gifts to sick people in town, Jews and gentiles alike.

As was usual in a Yiddish shtetl of Eastern Europe, there was a "hekdesh" in Drohichin. A hekdesh was a vacant house, where the many poverty-stricken Jews who wandered from town to town seeking tzedakah would spend their nights. Conditions in the hekdesh were awful. When Bobeh

Tzidkus Stands Forever

Henya would meet an ani in the street, she would say to him, "Please don't go to the hekdesh; come to my house." She would take these poor men home to sleep in her house. They would sleep on mattresses all over the floor.

Fire was one of the great terrors of the Eastern European shtetl. The small wooden houses stood close to each other, and firefighting methods and equipment were primitive or non-existent. It was not unknown for a raging fire to wipe out half of a town in a single occurrence.

Such a fire once broke out in Drohichin, and it consumed house after house as it roared down the street ever closer to the Perkovitzky home. My father's sister, Chana Malka, had memories of that fire, of the confusion and of people rushing back and forth to save things from the house. A relative, I think she said it was Moshe Shmuel, her father's younger brother, piled things into the carriage of the baby Cousin Faigel and rushed away with it, not noticing that the baby herself had fallen out of the carriage. My Tante Chana, not more than a child herself, cried out to him. He turned back, and she pointed to the baby Faigel lying in the snow. He scooped both of them into his arms and ran.

In the midst of all the fear and confusion, Bobeh Henya walked back and forth in the street, clapping her hands together in her emotion, and saying, "Ribono Shel Olam, not for my sake, but for the sake of all the poor people. If You wish, take everything I own; just leave over the house for the sake of all the poor people." The house was saved.

Tzidkus Stands Forever

My grandparents continued Bobeh Henya's practice of caring for others. My father told me that in his parents' home in Coney Island, people would simply knock on the door and ask "Is this Perr?" Then without any further ado, they would walk in, sit down at the table, and wait for something to eat.

And it was also continued in my parents' home, where homeless people would sometimes stay for months at a time. My parents always referred to these people as orchim, guests, an appellation of honor, rather than aniyim, the poor.

When my father was nine years old, he greatly surpassed the level of learning in the cheder of Drohichin. My father then wanted to leave home and to go away to learn in the yeshiva in Yanaveh. Yanaveh is located about 25 kilometers, or 15 miles, east of Drohichin. His mother was opposed to her only son, a mere child, leaving home. My father conducted a campaign of tears and entreaties, and he refused to eat, until my Bobeh Chaya Sloveh gave in.

Tzidkus Stands Forever

Although children in those times were far more mature and hardy than they are in our times, nevertheless, the willingness of a nine-year-old to leave the comforts of home and family in order to learn Torah has to be considered quite remarkable. It was especially so in my father's case, since he was by nature rather shy.

In those days, there were no dormitories. For meals, Yeshiva boys ate teg, eating at the houses of various Baalei Batim who were willing to take in a boy for a meal. My father told me that when he ate teg, "the soup was salty from my tears," so ashamed was he by the experience.

Around 1904, at the age of eleven, my father moved on from the yeshiva in Yaneveh to the yeshiva in Maltch. Maltch was yet further from home, at a distance of 48 kilometers, or 25 miles, northwest of Drohichin.

1903 had been an important year in Maltch. At the end of the winter, Rav Zalmen Sender Kahana Shapiro, the Rov and Rosh Yeshiva of Maltch, closed the yeshiva there which he himself had founded in 1898, and he moved with a small number of his talmidim to Krinik. Another group of talmidim remained on in Maltch, hoping that the yeshiva would be reopened. Before Shavuos, the good news was heard in Maltch that Rav Shimon Shkop had accepted the Rabbanus of the town and would be reopening the yeshiva. Indeed, Reb Shimon arrived before Rosh Hashana. Reb Shimon brought a number of talmidim with him, while another group was sent from Slabodka by the Alter. Still

Tzidkus Stands Forever

others were gathered from several other yeshivos. In all likelihood my father arrived, among those who came from other yeshivos.

When I was thinking about joining the Yeshiva of Philadelphia when it had just opened, my father encouraged me by telling me that the best years in a yeshiva are the first years after it opens. It is very likely that my father's experience in Maltch was the source of his advice.

In 1905, the civil unrest, which had long been brewing in Russia culminated in a full-fledged revolution, sparked by Russia's disastrous defeat at the hands of the Japanese. The revolution also made an impact within many of the yeshivos, and in Slabodka there was a serious rebellion against the Alter.

After Pesach in 1906, two brilliant youngsters aged 14 and 15 arrived in Slabodka. They would eventually become known as Rav Aharon Kotler and Rav Yaakov Kaminetzky. Sometime later, my father who was then around the age of bar mitzvah, arrived from Maltch.

When I arrived in Lakewood, the Rosh Yeshiva Reb Aharon told me that he remembered my father's arrival in Slabodka. "The olam had heard that a great baal kishron was coming," he said, "and there was much excitement when he arrived."

In those days, the Yeshiva Kneses Beis Yisroel in Slabodka attracted the greatest baalei kishron of

Tzidkus Stands Forever

Lita. According to what my Tante Chana told me, they went out of their way for my father in the yeshiva. They set him up to learn with chasanim, young men of marriageable age, as chaverusos; and in the festivities of that first Simchas Torah, someone carried him in the line with the Sifrei Torah, calling him "the little Sefer Torah." Although my father was in yeshiva during the same period of time as Reb Aharon and Reb Yaakov, and was close with both of them, the only chaverusa of my father in Slobodka whom I know of was Rav Yechezkel Halevi Berstein. Reb Yechezkel later became Rosh Yeshiva of the Yeshiva Ktana "Ohr Yisroel" in Slobodka. I found his sefer, Divrei Yechezkel, among my father's seforim. In those days, the sefer was unobtainable; however, far more important to me than the sefer itself was the dedication on the flyleaf of the volume, a beautiful expression of profound respect and caring from the author to my father. I once lent this precious sefer, with my father's permission, to an "older bochur" who had asked to borrow it. Unfortunately, it was never returned. Much later, I chanced to find it in a pile of discarded seforim. The covers and some pages were missing, and so was the flyleaf, with its precious dedication. Abjectly, I told my father what had happened. He didn't show the slightest interest or concern.

In 1912, Rav Isaac Scher, the son-in-law of the Alter, became Rosh Yeshiva of Slabodka. I once came across my father staring silently at a picture of Reb Isaac, hanging among other pictures of Gedolim in a classroom. "My Rebbe," my father said to me, as he turned slowly away. It was from

Tzidkus Stands Forever

Reb Isaac that my father received Semicha from Slabodka in 1925, when Reb Isaac was here in New York.

The only other time I heard my father mention Reb Isaac was when I asked him why he had so many of the various seforim of a certain mechaber. He told me, "Reb Isaac Scher held very much from his seforim. He told us to make sure to buy them if we ever had the opportunity."

I once asked my father if he had heard anything from the Alter of Slabodka about the machlokes that had occurred in 1905, shortly before he came to the yeshiva. My father answered, "No."

I then asked him, "Can you tell me something that you yourself heard from the Alter?"

He thought for a moment, and then he said, "Before bein hazmanim he used to say to us 'You are going home now, and you will be among simple, ordinary people in the shuls. Don't daven long Shmoneh Esrei's, don't shukle too much, don't do things that will seem strange to them.' Which means," my father said, "don't wear your tzitzis out either." And with that, he came back to something which he did not fully accept; the custom of American yeshiva bochurim, myself included, who were starting at that time, to wear their tzitzis outside their clothing. This was something which was not done by the European bnei torah.

My father's criticism of wearing one's tzitzis out was not derived from the fact that he hadn't seen this practice in

Tzidkus Stands Forever

Europe. My father was not at all committed to the way things had been, as the only way things must always remain. I believe that something more fundamental bothered him about this practice. What bothered him was a teaching of the Alter, which permeated all of Slobodka thinking and had shaped my father's thinking as well. The Alter taught that although "hachitzonius m'orar hapnimius" – the external, when practiced correctly, does indeed become internalized – nevertheless, it is also all too common for the external to become a substitute for the internal. The external can easily seduce a person into believing he has arrived at some elevated spiritual level, when he really has not.

When I came across a biography of Rav Mordechai Schulman, who was the Slabodka Rosh Yeshiva and the son-in-law of Rav Isaac Scher, I understood for the first time how much of my father's hashkafos and attitudes were a product of his years in Slabodka.

And with his leaving Slabodka, he did not sever his relationship with his yeshiva; he remained all his life a "Slabodka Yeshiva Talmid." Rav Mordechai Schulman and Rav Yosef Farber, grandsons of the Alter, were frequent guests in my father's home. Rav Nathan Lehrman, who at various times spent days and weeks at our home, was also a Slabodka talmid. And Rav Nosson Kaminetsky told me that while doing research for his book, he discovered that my father was the one Slabodka talmid in America who kept an

Tzidkus Stands Forever

ongoing contact with all the other Slabodka talmidim in this country.

Another Slabodka talmid with whom my father was very close in the 1920s was the founder of the first yeshiva in America where only Torah was studied, without general studies. This yeshiva in New Haven, Connecticut, was founded by Rav Yehuda Heshel Levenberg. Rav Levenberg was an extraordinary individual. He was, of course, a major Talmid Chachom, and he was also reputed to be the best rabbinical orator in America. Rav Levenberg considered Reb Itzel Peterburger to be his Rebbe. He had heard the shmuesin, which are printed in Ohr Yisrael, from Reb Itzel himself, and he would repeat them with the very same nigun that Reb Itzel had used at the time he delivered them.

Although eight years his junior, my father may have known Rav Levenberg yet from Europe. They shared a common history. They both had learned in Maltch, and they had both gone on to Slabodka. It is likely that it was during the years that he spent in Slabodka that Rav Levenberg became close with Reb Itzel. Reb Itzel left Slabodka for Eretz Yisroel in 1904.

My father may have visited Rav Levenberg in New Haven. He once said to me about Rav Levenberg, "I ate bread at his table for six years." By this he probably meant to say no more than he had been very close with him. When I asked him about Rav Levenberg's premature death at the age of 53, he didn't wish to talk about it. "A tragedy, a tragedy," was all

Tzidkus Stands Forever

he repeated over and over. Rav Hershel Levenberg, the son of Reb Yehuda Heshel, told me that my father is quoted a number of times in his father's unpublished manuscripts. To me, the most interesting thing about my father's connection with Rav Levenberg is that through him my father was, to a degree, also connected with Reb Itzel. Reb Itzel was a great mashpia, a great influence on the Alter of Navaradok, and also on the Alter of Slabodka. His sefer Ohr Yisroel, seems much more like what we understand Navaradok to have been, than what we understand Slabodka to have been. My father, although shaped by Slabodka, also contained much of what smacked of Navaradok

Rav Nosson Wachtfogel, mashgiach of Lakewood Yeshiva, once told me, "The Rosh Yeshiva speaks about your father like a chosid speaks about his Rebbe."

In later life, my father's reputation was that he was a tzadik. This reputation eclipsed his reputation as a talmid chachom. Rav Aharon Kotler told me several times about my father, "Ich halt ihm ainer fun de tzadikei hador – I hold him

Tzidkus Stands Forever

to be one of tzadikim of this generation." To others, I've been told, Reb Aharon said, "He is one of the 'thirty six' righteous men of this generation." And of course, a person does not suddenly become a tzadik in his old age. He had to have been at least something of a tzadik in his youth as well.

I remember meeting Chazan Mordechai Brooks in the beis medrash of the Yeshiva of Philadelphia, where I was a talmid at the time. Chazan Brooks was the father-in-law of Rav Shmuel Kaminetzky, and he was visiting his children in Philadelphia. His family had lived in Coney Island, and they had been close with my grandfather and his family, of whom he spoke glowingly. He then said to me, "I want you to know that your father was a tzadik from his earliest youth."

Because of my father's sterling reputation, he was approached with a number of lucrative offers to give hechsherim. My father lived through some very difficult economic times, but nevertheless he declined. However, many years later, he did supervise a relatively simple hechsher for the OU.

Rav Dov Schwartzman once told me that he was present when his father-in-law, Rav Aharon Kotler, was speaking to a certain rabbi about my father. Reb Aharon was telling this rabbi about my father's tzidkus, and he told him that my father refused to get involved with hechsherim. Reb Dov told me how surprised he was that Reb Aharon had said this to someone deeply involved in hechsherim. Reb Dov told me that the rabbi had in fact responded to Reb Aharon, "I do

Tzidkus Stands Forever

not see what is the greatness of such a thing!" However, in all likelihood, Reb Aharon said this to this rabbi, precisely because this rabbi was involved in hechsherim. By telling him about my father, Reb Aharon wanted the rabbi to hear that refraining from such heavy responsibilities and temptations to compromise, is indeed deserving of much praise.

Yet, although he refrained from hechsherim, my father never criticized someone else for giving a hechsher – even a hechsher that was considered not reliable. In those days, the OK Guide often published editorials castigating by name some rabbis who were giving unreliable hechsherim. I used to enjoy the sarcasm of those editorials. One time, my father overheard me laughing out loud over one of those editorials, and he stopped me short. He didn't like my participation in criticizing those Rabbis, even if it was merely by laughing.

In this, as in all that my father did, one never felt that he considered himself "holier than thou" about those who chose to act differently than he did. His attitude was that this just wasn't something that he wished to do.

His attitude reminds me very much of the answer "nisht kedai" which we talmidim frequently heard from Rav Aharon Kotler. People who were not close to Reb Aharon usually do not know that besides being a great gaon, he was also a great posek. But his talmidim knew full well that there was no question in the world about which he couldn't give a decisive p'sak. And we would ask him all sorts of sh'eilos.

Tzidkus Stands Forever

However, many times instead of answering "mutor" or "ossur," Reb Aharon would answer, "Es is nisht kedai – it is not worth it." This answer would leave us puzzled. What did the Rosh Yeshiva mean by the expression "not worth it"?

But "not worth it" is the answer of someone who is aware of what an aveira really is. When measuring what is to be gained by finding a leniency, against what may be lost by doing an aveira, it is just "not worth" following the lenient opinion. That is why my father did not give hechsherim. That is why Reb Aharon praised him for it.

Rav Yaakov Kamenetsky told me on a number of occasions, about the time when my grandfather, Rav Yosef Weinreb, had asked him about my father. Reb Yaakov had come to Toronto in 1938, and my grandfather asked him,

"You learned in Slabodka. Did you know someone in Slabodka named Mendel Perr?"

Reb Yaakov answered, "Yes, of course I knew him. He was 'zeher ah voiler' 'a very good person', but he has been here in America for many years now, and perhaps 'ehr is kalyeh gevoren!' 'Perhaps he has deteriorated!'"

My grandfather then said to him, "he is my son in-law!"

At this point in his story, Reb Yaakov would chuckle, and he would then say, "If I'd only known that he was asking

Tzidkus Stands Forever

about his son-in-law, I would never have suggested that perhaps he has deteriorated."

But that time when I asked Reb Yaakov if my father had always been a tzadik, and Reb Yaakov had answered that "he was always the same," he then went on to illustrate this by again telling me the same story, which he had already told me a number of times previously. This time however, he added something which he had never told me before. "Your grandfather then said to me, 'He is my son-in-law!' and then your grandfather added, 'Have no fear, he has definitely not deteriorated!' And when he said 'he has definitely not deteriorated,' I heard a tone of the deepest respect in your grandfather's voice. And your father, you understand, was just a young man then." And then Reb Yaakov added, "And don't forget; your grandfather was a Galitzianer, while your father was a Litvisher. And even though your grandfather had seen gedolim," which meant he had been exposed to great people, "still - he was a Galitzianer," Reb Yaakov continued, "and the definitions of tzidkus are very different between a Galitzianer and a Litvisher. And yet, he had such a profound respect for your father!"

My nephew Rav Yonoson Tendler was a first year high school student at the Yeshiva of Philadelphia when Rav Yaakov Kamenetsky once came to spend a Shabbos with his son Reb Shmuel. After the Friday night davening, the talmidim formed a line to extend a "gut Shabbos" to the

Tzidkus Stands Forever

rebbeim. As the young Yonoson passed, Reb Shmuel said to his father, "This is the grandson of Rav Perr."

Reb Yaakov rose to his feet and said, "It is not in your honor that I rise, but in honor of your grandfather and great-grandfather."

Over the years numerous people have said to me, "Oh, your father was such a tzadik!" And I always have the feeling that each of them was telling me something he had discovered by himself. For each of these people, it was an individual discovery, because my father did not fit today's stereotypes of how a tzadik is supposed to look. For most of his life, my father had no full beard. He did not dress in a bekesha or a homburg hat. He didn't insist on speaking Yiddish. For himself, and privately, he was extremely machmir in many things. For others, though, he searched for kulos. He never "dropped" the names of gedolim he knew, or whom he had known; and he never told anyone a story from which the listener could deduce something special about himself. Yet people from every walk of life who had some contact with him, who had seen how far he was willing to go to do the right thing and how great was his fear of sinning, each simply came to the conclusion on his own or her own that this man was a tzadik. Meeting him, for these people, was a great learning experience: a learning experience about what a Torah person is supposed to be.

Tzidkus Stands Forever

My grandfather lived alone in America for twelve years, until 1919, when he brought his family to New York. He returned to Europe a number of times during those twelve years to visit his family, but he refused my grandmother's entreaties to bring the family over to America; because, he said, America was not a place to raise children who will be Shomrei Torah and mitzvos.

However, the problem of Shmiras Hatorah did not stop him from helping others to emigrate. On one of his earliest return trips to Drohichin, he took a horse and wagon and rode around to all the nearby villages, seeking out the members of his extended family and asking them if they wished to immigrate to America. He was the one who eventually brought over all his cousins who were interested in immigrating. He "made papers" for them, getting them the necessary sponsors and visas, and he helped them with travel expenses. But his own family had to stay in Drohichin. America was no place for them.

In most cases, a man immigrated to America as a first step to eventually bringing over his family. My grandfather came here, only in order to support his family back home. There was no way to make a living in Eastern Europe. People were living in a poverty that was extreme and cruel. My grandfather, who listed his profession on his immigration papers as carpenter, found work in New York as an upholsterer.

Tzidkus Stands Forever

His specialty was reupholstering "lounges," a piece of furniture no longer used in our times. A lounge was a small, upholstered couch about five feet long and two feet wide. It was inclined at an angle with a built-in headrest at the high end. In those days, people lived cramped together in small apartments, and all the families on one floor shared a toilet in the hallway. With a lounge placed in the dining room, it was possible to take a nap while the bedrooms were being used by others.

Those twelve years alone in America were, of course, not easy years for my grandfather, and at some point, he brought over his oldest daughter, my Tante Chana Malka, to take care of him and to keep him company. My father said to me a number of times that his sister had the zechus of kibbud av.

After having been in New York for some time, my grandfather returned to Drohichin. By dint of hard work and by scrimping on his own living expenses, he brought back enough money to build a new house of thirteen rooms for his family. The house was built in such a way that seven to nine rooms could be rented out to tenants, in order to supplement the family income. The rest of the rooms were for the family's own use.

However, despite the newfound comfort of the family, my Bobeh still insisted that my grandfather take the family to America. According to what my father once told me, my Bobeh took my grandfather to the Drohichiner Rov. My

Tzidkus Stands Forever

Tante Chana, however, related that their going to the Rov came about differently; it was her father-in-law, Reb Mordechai, who took Bobeh to the Rov. He wanted the Rov to tell her that she was wrong in insisting that she wanted to immigrate to America.

At one point during their argument, Bobeh challenged Zeida with the question, "And how is it that you are able to be frum in America, tell me?"

My grandfather answered, "I am already grown up, but the children aren't." Besides being grown up, my grandfather had already successfully withstood the terrible nisyonos of serving four years in the Russian army.

Bobeh then said to Zeida, "Are you saying that it is absolutely impossible to raise frum children in America, or are you saying that it is a koontz – a difficult trick to pull off?"

"I'm saying that it's a koontz," Zaide was forced to admit.

"Well if it's a koontz," Bobeh said triumphantly, "then I want my chance to show that I can also make a koontz!"

According to my Tante Chana, the Rov remained silent and did not render a decision.

Eventually the family did come to America. Did Bobeh "make her koontz?" The answer for the most part is –

Tzidkus Stands Forever

yes. Despite the rush of her contemporaries to Americanization and modernization, she and her husband always remained the same as they had been in Drohichin. He was one of only a small number of Jews in America who wore a beard and she wore a sheitel. It was the only sheitel I had ever seen when I was a child.

Whenever I am reminded of it, I am always impressed by the strength of my grandfather's resolve not to expose his children to the almost insurmountable temptations of this country. And this was, despite the great physical and emotional toll upon himself, as well as upon them. And yet notwithstanding his obstinacy, my mother described her father-in-law as being a gentle, very caring person. A photograph of his family, which seems to have been taken around 1908, shows every member of his immediate family, except for him and my Tante Chana. It seems obvious that this picture was taken so that he might have it with him in far away America, to comfort him in his awful loneliness. And yet this ordinary working-man had the extraordinary commitment to Yiddishkeit that is to be expected of a great Talmid Chacham and Tzadik.

My father told me two things about his father at different times, and I believe that I detected a hint of pride in his voice when he told these things to me. He told me that my grandfather died without leaving over any debts. For an immigrant who had worked his way up, who had brought over all his family and relatives, and who had lived through

Tzidkus Stands Forever

the Great Depression of the 1930s, I'm sure that not leaving over debts was not only a great accomplishment, but also a reflection of his deep honesty.

The other thing my father mentioned was that his father had served for four years in the Russian Army and he had never eaten anything treif during those four years. I do not understand how he did this. There were no Jewish chaplains to help the soldiers. There was no canned kosher food that could be sent from home. And in Russia, there was no decent treatment for Jews, even Jewish soldiers. It is impossible for us who live here in America, to comprehend the degree of self-sacrifice that was required in order not to eat anything treif for those four years.

I remember one visit to my grandmother in Coney Island. At the time, I was in the third year of the Beis Medrash at Mesivta Rabbi Chaim Berlin. My grandmother always gave me special attention, and many times she would ask me which mesechta I was learning. This time, I answered, "Baba Kama," and she nodded; she recognized the names of the various masechtos. I was learning by Rav Aharon Soloveichik at the time, and it occurred to me that she might know the name. "You know, Bobeh," I said, "my Rebbi's name is Reb Aharon Soloveichik."

"Soloveichik?" she asked with surprise, "is he perhaps the son of Reb Chaim?"

"Not the son," I answered, "the grandson."

Tzidkus Stands Forever

"A grandson, and he is your chavrusa?" she asked.

"Not my chavrusa, Bobeh, my Rebbi," I answered.

"Reb Chaim has already a grandson who is old enough to be your Rebbe?" she asked with astonishment. "Could this be?"

I resisted the urge to tell her that Reb Aharon had even older brothers, and instead I asked her if she remembered Reb Chaim.

"Of course I remember Reb Chaim!" she hastened to assure me, "but Reb Yoshe Ber, oy Reb Yoshe Ber, was he a tzadik, such a tzadik!" and she clasped her hands and moved her head from side to side, as the memory of him flowed over her.

When I told my father how much more moved his mother had been by the memory of Reb Yoshe Ber than by that of Reb Chaim, he told me that Reb Chaim had once said himself that he knew he would never be as beloved as his father had been.

Later on, my father told me that during the four years that his father was in the Russian army, my grandmother worked in the house of Reb Yoshe Ber in Brisk. "Oh," I said, "she was a maid."

Tzidkus Stands Forever

"Not a maid!" my father said, a little hurt by the word. "She helped out in the house with the children and other such things."

How my Bobeh came to the home of Reb Yoshe Ber is something my father did not know, but he thought that there may have been some distant familial connection to the Soloveichiks.

The outbreak of the First World War changed everyone's plans. My father, who was learning in Slabodka, was called home by his mother, probably in 1916. He spent the next few years learning in Drohichin, where, as he told me himself, he could in no way replicate his Yeshiva learning. The Slabodka Yeshiva was forced to move deeper into Russia, to Minsk, and its talmidim scattered. The shtetlach were stalked by starvation and by the depredations and the many murders of Jews committed by the Cossacks.

In this new situation, my grandfather gave in at last and brought his family to America.

In celebration of the arrival of his family, he planned a special treat. Oranges were a rare and exotic fruit in Eastern Europe. My grandfather had once given my father an orange as a birthday present. I believe it was for his ninth birthday.

Now, having picked up his family from Ellis Island, and having settled them in the apartment he had rented for them at 171 Broome Street on the Lower East Side, my

Tzidkus Stands Forever

grandfather disappeared for a few minutes, only to return shortly after with a whole basket of oranges. He set the basket down on the table in front of his amazed children. "Here," he said happily, "eat!"

Two years later, the family settled in Coney Island. The backyard of their new home at 2837 W. 24th Street was entirely taken up with a bungalow, which served as a rental to those who spent the summer in Coney Island in order to escape the unbearable heat of the city.

Renting out space made it possible for my grandfather to afford the new house he had built years earlier in Drohichin. I would venture that he chose to live in Coney Island, so that he would be able to rent out space to help him pay for this house as well.

My grandfather's activities, however, were not limited to the welfare of his own family. Not long after he bought his new house in Coney Island, he undertook a

Tzidkus Stands Forever

massive and all-absorbing project. Near my grandparents' home lived Rav Aryeh Leib Ralbag. Rav Ralbag was from Yerushalayim and had the reputation of being very frum. My father spent a lot of time in the Ralbag home. Seforim were very expensive and rare in those days before modern printing methods, and Rav Ralbag possessed an extensive library. Whenever my father was not in yeshiva, he was to be found in Rav Ralbag's library, immersed in his seforim at all hours.

Sometime in the 1920s, Rav Ralbag had a disagreement with the baalei batim of his shul, Congregation Shaarei Tzedek, located on Mermaid Avenue at the corner of West 23rd street. The president of the shul took the Rabbi's shtender and his tallis and carried them out from the shul into the front foyer. My grandfather came over to Rav Ralbag and said to him, "Rebbe, don't be afraid, I will build another shul for you."

Rav Ralbag, however, told my grandfather that Coney Island must also have a mikvah. Thereupon, my grandfather undertook the immense task of building the mikvah of Coney Island in addition to a shul for Rav Ralbag. The shul and mikvah were located next to each other on West 25th Street, between Mermaid and Surf Avenues. The shul bore the legal name "Orthodox Congregation of Coney Island." What it was called by the yidden seems to have been Beis Hamedrash Horav.

To me as a youngster, my Bobeh's house in Coney Island was an exotic and mysterious place. I loved examining

Tzidkus Stands Forever

all its nooks and crannies. Once on a visit, I happened to pull open a drawer, and was surprised to find it packed full of black buttons, all the same size. When I asked my Tante Chava Bluth about the buttons she laughed, and said "Tatele," the name I was called by all my aunts, "they're for 'piece work'." My Tante Chana then explained; what did my aunts do before they were married, in the evenings or whenever else they were free? They sat and stitched rows of these buttons neatly onto cards. These cards were turned over to a distributor, and eventually they were sold in various stores. Each card brought in a little something for the family.

In the 1920s, the U.S. Department of Labor mandated a 54-hour work week for factory workers. That was nine hours a day for six days a week. An immigrant without a secular education or financial resources had to work in a sweatshop or some other business where he was expected to work on Shabbos. On Sunday, all factories and businesses were closed. The few who refused to work on Shabbos faced a great struggle in order to scratch out a living for their families. Any family member who was capable was expected to help alleviate the family's heavy burden. Besides helping his family, a son was also expected to prepare himself to eventually support his own family.

Yet in my father's family, there was no question about what he should be doing. His sisters would do "piece work," but my father would be learning at the premier Torah

Tzidkus Stands Forever

institution of that time, which was then located on the Lower East Side, Yeshivas Rabbeinu Yitzchok Elchonon.

In those days, with the exception of Navaradok, all the great Yeshivos of Europe prepared their talmidim to become Rabbonim. Rabbanus was not the most lucrative pursuit by any means, but one could remain close to Torah and usually make at least a meager living through it. My father's idealism, scholarship, love for learning, and strength of character made him an excellent candidate for the Rabbanus. But if not for his family's attitude and their support for him in those lean years of struggle, he could never have been among the handful, out of hundreds of thousands of Eastern European immigrants, who was to be found learning in a yeshiva.

In a photograph of the musmachim of 1923, my father stands in the second row. Seated in the first row, coincidently, is his future mechutan Rav Isaac Tendler.

The few years that my father was at the Yeshiva provided him with the opportunity not only to learn, but also to get to know, and to be known by, the prominent Rabbonim and Torah personalities of the time. He also learned to speak fluent English, and he became a good public speaker. These skills would later serve him well in his life's mission.

It also provided him with a comeback which he enjoyed very much. When he and I would debate some

Tzidkus Stands Forever

halacha issue, and he happened to take the lenient view, he would often then say to me, "What do you expect, Yechiel? You know that I am a Y.U. man!" I would wince at this joke, but he would then pause, and his face would crinkle into a smile.

It was about his first Rabbanus that my father spoke, when he told me that after his first year there the baalei batim told him that they were not going to renew his contract. My father said to them, "You are my first shul and I am your first Rov. What will you do now? You will contact Yeshivas Rabbeinu Yitzchok Elchonon, and they will send you someone else who will also be a Rov for the first time. At the very least, let me suggest someone to you who already has a year's experience!"

"Who is this person?" they asked.

"It is me!" my father answered.

"They liked what I said very much," my father told me, "and they agreed that I should stay on for another year.

Tzidkus Stands Forever

When the end of the second year came, they asked me to stay on longer. 'No,' I said, 'now I'm going!' I just did not want to be sent away," my father told me.

Where this, his first Rabbanus had been, he did not wish to tell me. But it was in Rochester, New York. He was the Rov of Mercaz Bais Yehuda, Beth Jehuda Center, and he lived at 1150 St. Paul Street. On his personal stationary that he had printed at the time, he wrote "Rav Lekehillas Yeshurun." In this title, one can detect his sense of responsibility as a Rov for our ancient Klal Yisroel. And his choice of the name "Yeshurun" refers to the straightness for which Klal Yisroel is praised, and which he himself so abundantly possessed.

What my father was like as a Rov can be understood from what I was told about his second Rabbanus, in Mount Carmel, Pennsylvania.

I had a conversation with Oscar Coren of Dunbar Street in Bayswater, N.Y, in 1988. Mr. Coren told me that my father became the Rov of Mount Carmel in 1926, the year before Mr. Coren became bar mitzvah. Mount Carmel was at that time a town of 40 Jewish families, with a shul that had been built in 1924 or 1925. My father lived in a little house next door to the shul, and he had his meals at the Coren home, which was four houses away from the shul. He received a salary of 1500 dollars a year. The Coren family bakery was six doors away from the shul, and Oscar Coren's

Tzidkus Stands Forever

father, together with his sons, made up the minyan of the shul. My father usually led the davening.

My father was still single, and Oscar Coren remembered that my father stayed on in Mount Carmel for five or six years. Mr. Coren's description of my father in those years shows that he never really changed. Even as a young man, he possessed the same qualities that made him so special at an older age. Mr. Coren said about my father, "He was always busy. He was always willing to teach. He was very interested in teaching children. The cheder had 25 or 30 kids among the 40 families. We loved him. He was a kind, soft-spoken gentleman. Our family had eight children. We sat around the table, and he would talk with us. He taught three classes a day in the cheder. He gave me a job to take around a lulav and esrog the whole week of Succos. He paid me a quarter for the week. He was a real talmid chochom! I remember that he shaved with a depilatory. He was a meticulous person about himself. And he was a thin person."

It is interesting that Oscar Coren, who was a youngster at the time, would know how my father shaved. A photograph taken at a studio in Mount Carmel at that time shows my father as a dapper, well-dressed young man with his hair parted in the middle in the style of the times. How would he have allowed his young student to watch him while he shaved?

Knowing my father, the answer is quite simple. In those days, the majority of baalei batim shaved with razors.

Tzidkus Stands Forever

Even after the Schick shaver became available, this deeply ingrained and widespread practice did not cease. Until his later years, my father always shaved with a depilatory, "powder" he called it. Many frum men bought a ready-made depilatory for shaving. But my father would buy a jar of a certain type of sulfur at a drug store, and some "whiting," the ingredient in white-wash, at a hardware store. He would mix the two in a certain proportion, make a paste with water, and smear it on his face. In five or ten minutes, he would scrape it off with what he called "a bone," a hard rubber spatula. To protect his clothes, he would tuck a sheet of newspaper in his collar, and let it hang down the front of his shirt.

In the 1950's, my father taught at Yeshiva Heichal Hatorah for two years. The Yeshiva was founded by Rabbis Yaakov and Yechiel London, to teach those who had not had a previous Torah education. At twelve o'clock on Fridays my father would shave with powder at the yeshiva, and he would show the boys how he did it, so that they would follow his example. There is no question, that my dapper young father was already demonstrating the permitted method of shaving for his young charges in Mt. Carmel, years earlier.

Years later in South Ozone Park, my father would buy Schick shavers and give them to individuals who promised him that they would use them. He obtained the shavers at a discount price; even so, they still cost him 14 dollars each. Fourteen dollars was a large percentage of his weekly

Tzidkus Stands Forever

salary. My father had reservations about the kashrus of the shaver, but he thought it certainly was preferable to a razor. However, he then discussed the matter with Rav Aharon Kotler, who was opposed to using a shaver at all. Reb Aharon dissuaded him from continuing the practice.

The Saturday morning edition of the Schenectady Gazette on August 31, 1929 carried an item captioned, "Rabbi Perr to speak at Agudah Synagogue." The item went on to tell us that Rabbi Menachem Perr would officiate at two Bar Mitzvahs and speak twice. In the morning, he would speak on "the Jewish answer to the recent occurrence in Palestine," no doubt referring to the atrocious massacre which the Arabs had perpetrated in Chevron a few days earlier on August 23rd and 24th. At six o'clock in the afternoon he would speak again, this time on "Unity and strength in our ranks."

Someone's imagination had contributed to the item that my father was a graduate of City College and of New York Theological Seminary. My father had never attended even an elementary school, and he also had semicha was from Yeshiva Rav Yitzchok Elchonon. However, the rest of the item is no doubt accurate. What my father was doing in Schenectady that Shabbos, we will never know. Perhaps he was trying out for a Rabbonus at Agudas Achim, or perhaps he had some connection with the family of one of the Bar Mitzvah boys. It is clear, however, that the topics he chose to speak on were topical and inspirational.

Tzidkus Stands Forever

Also, sometime in 1929, my father returned to his parents' home in Coney Island. Why he left Mount Carmel, we will never know. Perhaps he wanted to be in New York in order to more easily find a shidduch.

In the early 1930s my parents were introduced to each other through mutual friends. My mother had difficulty deciding about the shidduch. My father was so different from her own father, he was so Litvish! She called her father in Toronto to discuss it with him. When she told her father of her hesitations, he responded in his Galitzianer Yiddish "Uber her shaimt-zich fahr ah talmid chuchom," "but he has a reputation as a talmid chachom!" And indeed my father had established a reputation for his learning in the New York of the 1920s and 1930s.

My father's being a recognized talmid chachom was the prime factor in my grandfather's decision in favor of the marriage. As my mother later told me, it was in my mother's as well.

Tzidkus Stands Forever

My father was involved with giving lectures at the Young Israel of Eastern Parkway and at the Young Israel of Boro Park, as well as at other shuls.

The Young Israel movement at that time was the only national organization for strengthening yiddishkeit and fighting the forces of assimilation. My father's Torah lectures and articles in the Young Israel publications made him a leader in this effort. In appreciation, the Young Israel of Boro Park gave him a beautiful besamim holder as a gift on the occasion of his marriage. On Tuesday, the 21st of Elul, September 12th, 1933, at five o'clock in the afternoon, my father and mother were married at Hoffman Mansion, 50-01 15th Avenue, Brooklyn, NY. Dinner followed the ceremony.

It is no longer possible to know for sure why the wedding was held in Brooklyn and not in Toronto. It's possible that there was no catering facility in Toronto at that time whose kashrus my grandfather was willing to endorse by making a wedding there. His many years of battles for kashrus would culminate five years later with an announcement in the Toronto Yiddish Journal of November 11th 1938 that "no kosher meat is to be found in Toronto." This statement was signed by seven rabbonim, headed by my grandfather.

There may also have been another, sadder reason why the wedding was held in New York. It is very possible that the wedding, or a large part of it, was paid for by my father, or by his father. Although my grandfather had been

Tzidkus Stands Forever

brought to Toronto from Europe to serve as the Rov, his community was not paying his salary, or at least a good part of it. It is possible that the community was very poor, especially after the great financial crash of 1929. However, it may also have been a reaction to my grandfather's uncompromising stand in marginalizing mechalelei Shabbos in the community and his insistence on rigorous kashrus standards.

Because of this, the Rov lived in a dignified genteel poverty, and it is possible that he couldn't afford to make a wedding in Toronto. If this is true, then it's very likely that my father or my grandfather paid for the wedding, and therefore they made it in New York.

Whatever the reason, the wedding was held in Brooklyn. In the manner of weddings at that time, there were speeches and toasts at the wedding dinner. The master of ceremonies was Mr. Irving Bunim, with whom my father was very close at that time, no doubt through his involvement with the Young Israel movement.

My father in those days spoke an impeccable English, with a trace of an accent which gave his speech a special chein. He was thin, as he was to remain throughout his life, and he was well-dressed in the fashion of the times.

Tzidkus Stands Forever

The 1930s were a very difficult time financially. The stock market crash in 1929 had led to a collapse of the whole economy. The country was in a deep depression. Nearly 12 million people were unemployed.

The Depression was not an easy time for my parents as well. For a while, my father had a position in a shul on Avenue D in Flatbush. When that position came to an end, my father was unemployed for some months, a fact which my mother was embarrassed to share even with her own father. Of course, my father was always a very active person, and he continued his activities during that time as well. As he had been doing since he returned to New York he wrote articles, he taught classes, he lectured, he was mekarev, and above all, he learned. I know that at some point in time, my father also gave a shiur at Yeshiva Rav Yitzchok Elchonon. This was probably also at that time, during the 1930s.

On the twenty-fifth of Adar I in 1935, my grandfather Yechiel Yitzchok Perr passed away at the age of 67. He was an active and vital person, but he had a problem with his heart. My Tante Chana was in Eretz Yisroel at the time, and she was mispallel for her father at the grave of her grandmother, her mother's mother, Yehudis, on Har Hazeisim. She also "measured out" the kever with a string, and sent the string to New York to be wrapped around the sick man. But all this was to no avail. He died, and the family was devastated. He was buried close to the grave of someone whom he admired as a true tzadik. My grandfather

Tzidkus Stands Forever

had joined the chevra kadisha with the condition that he be buried near that person.

In 1939, four years after my grandfather died, his own father, Reb Mordechai Zhaluzher, passed away in Drohichin at the age of 88. He had always lived together with my father and his sisters, and he was really like a second father to them. I once came across a letter from the Rov of Drohichin to my father, in which he gave an account of how Reb Mordechai passed away. When my father saw me reading it, he took it away from me. It seems the account it contained was too personal to be shared with anyone else. It was Reb Mordechai who adopted the name Perkovitzky. My father told me that originally the family name had been Pomerance. There were several brothers in the family, and to avoid the army Reb Mordechai went to live with a childless uncle and took his name, Perkovitzky. An only son was not drafted into the army. According to my father's best guess, Zhaluzhe was the name of some very small village, a "derful," where his grandfather had lived for a while. Except for this, the family had lived in Drohichin continuously for several hundred years. Three months after my grandfather's death in 1935, I, their first child, was born to my parents. Some months later, my father took a trip out to Queens to apply for a vacant rabbanus on behalf of his brother-in-law Reb Shmuel Lew, husband of his sister Fradle. The committee with whom he met could not be swayed in favor of my uncle Reb Shmuel, but they were interested in my father. And so, towards the end of 1935, my father became the Rov of South

Tzidkus Stands Forever

Ozone Park, a position he was to occupy for the rest of his life. It was there that my sister Esther Tendler and my brother Rav Eliezer were born and raised. It was South Ozone Park that would be the focus of his activities and the base from which he would stretch out his hands in kiruv to any other Jew whom he could reach.

South Ozone Park is located more to the east than to the south of Ozone Park. It was named South Ozone Park because the developers built it after they had already built Ozone Park. It seems that at that time, before the Department of Health ever broadcast an ozone alert, ozone was considered a good thing to breathe. "Ozone Park" was an attractive name that sounded like "fresh air" to families living in Manhattan and Brooklyn. And having come up with such an attractive name as "Ozone Park" the developers intended to milk it for all it was worth. Thus, the name "South Ozone Park."

Tzidkus Stands Forever

South Queens is built up almost entirely with small, one family homes. The acquisition of such a home represented the fulfillment of the "American Dream" for the thousands of mostly second generation Italians who made up the majority of the population.

The main thoroughfare of the South Queens communities is crowned with a name, no doubt chosen in order to add an aura of class; even luxury; and perhaps even high culture; to the blessing of good health bestowed upon the fortunate citizens by the ozone. It is called "Rockaway Boulevard."

Rockaway Boulevard is lined up and down with "mom and pop" stores whose proprietors in those years were very often second-generation immigrant Jews. These Jews had also acquired "American Dream" one-family houses, and they lived sprinkled two or three to a block, among their Italian neighbors, throughout the area. Their children were enrolled at P.S. 96 and P.S. 155, from where they graduated and went on to attend John Adams High School.

In 1923, the Jews of South Ozone Park organized themselves into a community. In 1925, they erected a shul building and retained their first Rabbi, Rabbi Hyman Barras. At the time my father became the Rov, there were only a few Shomer Shabbos families. The ones whom I remember were the Leifers, the Schnecks and the Willners. Mr. Willner was a very fine European-born man who owned the butcher store

Tzidkus Stands Forever

in town. He was our butcher all the years. His children and grandchildren are all Shomrei Shabbos until this day.

But most of the other Jewish people were not Shomrei Shabbos. They were storekeepers for the most part, and stores were open on Shabbos, and were required by law to be closed on Sunday. But they were people who were deeply aware of being Jewish. They were afraid of anti-Semitism, and therefore of being conspicuously Jewish. They wanted their sons to be Bar Mitzvah and to marry Jewish girls. They went to shul on Rosh Hashanah and Yom Kippur, and usually whenever yizkor was said. Most of them understood, and some could even speak some Yiddish. Most could read Hebrew, and they said kaddish for their parents. Most of their wives bought kosher meat from Mr. Willner, or perhaps from a less reliably kosher butcher. They knew about milchigs and fleishigs, although they were not scrupulous when a mix up occurred. Some had been influenced by the apikorsus in the Yiddish papers, or in the world around them, and also by the letzonus of the Yiddish theater.

But for the most part they were simple, good people, who belonged to the shul, who didn't daven but came to shul meetings. Who sent their kids to public school, but also to the Talmud Torah, and who hadn't the slightest idea that they were to be the last generation of Jews in their families; that their children were to become the famous "lost generation," whose own children for the most part, would cease to be Jews entirely.

Tzidkus Stands Forever

My father's most intensive efforts were with the young. He taught the classes at the shul's Talmud Torah. With the better boys, he would learn mishnayos, especially Bava Metzia. With a very few, he was able to learn Gemara. But to all of them he would teach Chumash and Sefer Shmuel, into which he poured his heart and his love for yiddishkeit. He was filled to overflowing with the explanations of the meforshim as well as with his own special insights, but he was careful not to overload his talmidim with different opinions. In order for them to hear the Torah's message clearly, he would teach only one interpretation. And he chose always to give explanations that were understandable and inspiring to his students. He avoided the explanations that they might find irrational, or mysterious.

My father understood that the Torah wants us not only to learn, but also to be inspired by the actions of our forefathers, by their truthfulness, and their sacrifices and their greatness. He believed that the impact of the Chumash becomes obscured and muted when too many opinions about what happened are presented, or when, what are to the students, poorly understood and "mystical" midrashim are added.

Throughout his life, he learned Chumash and he puzzled over the p'shat. The heroes of the Torah were as alive to him, and because of him, as alive in our home, as if they were members of our family who were perhaps only absent at the moment. For several years he learned with me

Tzidkus Stands Forever

at home every day in the morning, and among other things, we completed the Chumash. I will never forget how he cried when he taught me the parsha of the death of Moshe Rabbeinu. As I write these words, my own eyes are filled with tears. Nor can I avoid tears when that parsha is read on Simchas Torah; all from the memory of my father's tears.

Having had the privilege of such an experience made it easy for me to understand the usage we find of olov hashalom when mentioning the name of Moshe Rabbeinu. The use of this expression is usually reserved for someone we knew personally. My father did not say olov hashalom about Moshe Rabbeinu. But after the experience of watching him cry, I could easily understand using this expression.

Another important thing that I learned from my father is that there was no "skipping" any part of the Torah. Every word, every letter is inestimably important. The lists of generations in Bereishis were learned and reviewed and the numbers added up laboriously on paper. The mishkan was studied and every vessel carefully examined. The details of the karbonos in Vayikra were memorized. The chapter of Yehuda and Tamar was learned like every other, with no embarrassment or censorship.

My father once found out that a certain Yeshiva started using a Chumash text that had been abridged by some self-anointed pedagogical expert. He went down to the Yeshiva and made sure that those text books were removed. To this day I am astonished when I hear that certain frum

Tzidkus Stands Forever

mosdos skip parts of the Chumash, supposedly for the benefit of their students.

Teaching Talmud Torah was surely not easy for my father. The youngsters had been in public school until three o'clock. Then, finally freed from school, they had to spend another hour or more in Talmud Torah, where they were supposed to behave while learning and being drilled in reading and translation of an unfamiliar and difficult language. Meanwhile, all their friends from public school were outside playing ball, riding their bikes, or playing in the snow. There were times when I substituted for my father, teaching at the Talmud Torah. I know what he went through all those years.

It is a profound tribute to my father's dedication, his sincerity, and his ability to inspire, that he was able to reach and inspire many of those youngsters under such difficult conditions. But for him, the key to winning a child was Shabbos. The most important thing was to get him to come daven at least on Shabbos morning, and then to spend as

Tzidkus Stands Forever

much of the Shabbos as possible in the shul; this would keep the child away from the ordinary day that Saturday was, both in the outside world and in his own home.

As far back as I can remember, a number of the youngsters who came to shul on Shabbos would almost always eat at our home afterwards. My mother was an excellent cook, and the kids went to work on her meals with gusto. Of course, there were also zemiros, and brochos, and bentching. Some of those kids were real characters, and difficult to bear, but that was never a consideration. I have no idea how my parents managed to do this financially. But my mother was very frugal in every other way; she knew very well how to stretch a dollar. I never once heard my mother complain about the expense or trouble involved. She considered it to be her responsibility as much as my father considered it to be his.

There were times, as I was growing up, that I secretly objected to not ever having the privacy of just our own family at the Shabbos meals. But I knew that what my parents were doing was right, and neither I, nor my sister or brother ever complained about it.

Inviting youngsters for the Shabbos meal was something my father did throughout his life. But there were parents who were adamantly against their children becoming frum.

Tzidkus Stands Forever

One parent told my father that he doesn't want his son to be a fanatic, "That means someone more religious than you!" my father answered.

Etched in my memory is a scene of a nine or ten year old youngster, a friend of mine, standing in the front hall of the shul, sobbing loudly and asking my father between gasps, "If you have to break the Fourth Commandment or the Fifth, which one should you break?"

My father answered him, "First you must keep the Fourth Commandment. Then, if it is possible, you also keep the Fifth." This youngster had just been forced, screaming, by his father into an automobile, and had then been driven around the block on Shabbos to "knock the nonsense out of his head." After many years of struggle, not only did he remain frum, his parents finally became observant also.

In the case of another youngster, my father would stand for hours on Shabbos afternoons outside his father's store, waiting for the boy to be sent on an errand, so that he could "catch" him, and take him away to the shul. My father would stand there even in the rain. This youngster is today the father and grandfather of a large Torah family.

There were a number of others who also became and remain, at the very least, Shomrei Shabbos. A larger number still were observant at least for a while. They surely have retained at least a positive attitude about being frum.

Tzidkus Stands Forever

Shabbos afternoon was spent "downstairs" in the shul. There was a homemade Ping-Pong table there, and a good part of the afternoon was spent absorbed in this sport. Later, a homemade knock hockey game was also brought in. Knock hockey is a game in which two or four players moved a pingpong ball to a goal by rotating sticks with small pegs in them. At some point in the afternoon, my father would come down and tell us it was time to learn. We would follow him upstairs to learn some Chumash and Mishnayos.

Then there was a shalosh seudos, with pickled herring or gefilte fish balls, soda, and cake, and with zemiros in the gathering dusk. This is how the Shabbos was spent by the more committed youngsters.

One of the frummest boys was learning in a Yeshiva. He was one of the very few, over the years, who went on to learn in a Yeshiva. He came to my father and told him that his Rebbi had said that it is not permissible to play Ping Pong on Shabbos. I remember my father saying to him, "That's all right. That's all right. I take the aveira upon myself. No one else will be punished for it. Don't stop the others from playing."

There were several reasons why almost none of the boys ended up attending a Yeshiva. First, there were very few Yeshivas in New York, and none at all in our neighborhood. Also, the parents did not want their children "to become Rabbis." In addition, some of the few that my father had sent to Yeshiva earlier on did not adjust to the Yeshivas, and they

Tzidkus Stands Forever

became disillusioned with yiddishkeit. Because of this my father did not easily agree to send a good boy off to a Yeshiva. Sadly, large numbers of the Talmud Torah children would just disappear after they were Bar Mitzvah despite all my father's efforts. The more serious and idealistic ones, would continue their personal relationship with my father, and would continue learning with him, often one on one.

The girls, too, were not ignored. My mother had "her girls" whom she taught and worked with. They were a smaller number than the boys, but many of them have remained loyal Jews, and a few of them even became frum. This much may be said of them and of the boys also; at the very least, whoever went through my father's hands would know for the rest of his life that he or she was a Jew, and that G-d expected something from him or her.

Tzidkus Stands Forever

Intermarriage was without question the most painful and tragic event in my father's experience; unfortunately, it was a more frequent one as time went on. My father tried very hard to keep contact with the young people. For a while, he was able to have a Sunday morning minyan for the teenage boys. Whenever my father would speak to one of his former students, he continued to use his Hebrew name, just as he had done in Talmud Torah. The kids would call it "my Jewish name." For them, it was the name that signified to them they were Jewish. But these youngsters also attended public high school. This was the generation that went on after high school to college, not store keeping and the gentile girls wanted them. Their mothers told them to try and catch a nice Jewish boy. A Jewish boy meant a long-term marriage to a good earner, someone who didn't beat his wife.

In that generation, when there was intermarriage on the horizon, the parents were invariably heartbroken, and they would come to my father for help. My father would try his best. One boy named Alan returned from college in Miami, where he was studying music, engaged to a Gentile girl. Alan's family had once lived upstairs from us in the house where we had previously lived. Alan was just a few years older than me, and he was my friend. Alan's grandmother, Mrs. Epstein, was a Yiddish speaking woman. Alan's father, Moe, was a taciturn man with a florid complexion, who was a partner with his brother in M&M Auto Sales, where he sold used cars. I don't remember him ever being in shul.

Tzidkus Stands Forever

Shortly afterwards, Alan's father, Moe, began coming to shul Friday night. There no longer was a minyan on Friday nights, just a few Yidden davening together beyechidus. But there was Moe, holding a Hebrew-English siddur, and quietly following along. He sat apart from the others, on a bench almost in the back of the shul. It was as if he was saying that he really didn't belong here, because he hadn't come all of those years.

Of course, my father must have told Moe that his lack of interest in yiddishkeit was the reason that Alan was marrying a gentile girl. This led to Moe's starting to come on Friday nights. Moe never came Shabbos morning because of the business. But if my father could get a Jew to keep part of the Shabbos he knew he had accomplished a great deal.

In another case, my father took a boy's father to see the Bobover Rebbe. Probably, this person had come from a Bobover family. I had the pleasure of being taken along, and we were taken to the head of the line of the waiting Chasidim. The Rebbe was especially nice to me, and he showed me a picture taken during the war of himself in a military uniform and without a beard. Half a century later, I met the Rebbe again and told him that he had shown me the picture.

In another case, my father tried to gain the cooperation of the local priest, Father Fusco of Saint

Tzidkus Stands Forever

Anthony's. Fusco agreed that he would try to convince the girl not to marry, while my father would try to convince the boy not to marry. The priest spoke to the girl, extracted a promise from her that she would raise her children as Catholics, and then he dropped the matter. When my father called Fusco to complain that he hadn't kept his end of the bargain, Fusco answered him, "Why should I care, Rabbi? My own Bishop has a Jewish mother."

Around 1946, one of my father's very close students suggested forming a Shomer Shabbos Boy Scout troop as a way of connecting the local boys with the shul. My father thought it over and then decided it was a good idea. The war had brought about a great enthusiasm for uniforms. All the kids were wearing various khaki shirts and soldier hats; some of the really lucky ones even wore whole outfits of khaki. The Boy Scouts was an "in thing" with the kids, and if they didn't have their own troop, they would join a gentile troop without question.

Our shul, however, was unable to put together its own troop. In the end, our kids formed their own patrol as part of a Shomer Shabbos troop in Ozone Park. The shul's patrol lasted for about two years. Two men, who are today Bnei Torah, were helped along the way by that Boy Scout troop, although not by our patrol. But the patrol did provide the youngsters from the shul with an incomparably better seviva than they would have had otherwise.

Tzidkus Stands Forever

When Rav Shneur Kotler came to be menachem avel during my father's shiva, he told me that his father, Reb Aharon, was here in New York in 1936. My father used the opportunity of Reb Aharon's visit to renew his relationship with him. He also received a semicha from Reb Aharon at that time. It is well known that Reb Aharon gave only a very few semichas. The semicha he gave my father was the personal semicha that has been given from time immemorial; it was a semicha that speaks of the qualities of the one to whom the semicha is being given. The semicha is undated; what follows is my translation.

"It is my intention with this, to bring recognition to my honored friend, the eminent Rov, a bright and expert storehouse of Torah and of the fear of Heaven, Moreinu Horav Menachem Mendel Perr; a person whom I have known very well from his youth, when he was already known for his abilities, for his unusual success in his studies both in factual knowledge and in sharp analysis, and for his understanding of matters in a very straight manner.

At this time, while in the United States, I had the pleasure of discussing with him, on a number of occasions, G-

Tzidkus Stands Forever

d's word: Halacha. And I have found that he has grown to be very great in Torah; that he understands how to arrive at a new decision based on previous decisions; and that he knows how to extract the correct Halacha from the Talmudic discussion. And now, since he is also exceptional in his Yiras Shomayim, and in Daas Torah, and since he also has precious Midos, I join my hand with his, and grant him the semicha of our Sages, Yoreh Yoreh Yadin Yadin to be a Rav and decider of law and Torah: for he is fit to lead G-d's community to the wellsprings of Torah and fear of Heaven. And it is my hope and expectation that with his diligence in Torah study, he will surely continue to rise ever upwards in G-ds Torah, in the future. I write this and affix my signature in order to bring honor to the Torah and to those who study it. Aharon Kotler. The relationship of my father and Reb Aharon, which had begun in Slabodka and which was renewed in 1936, would culminate five years later, when Reb Aharon arrived in the United States, into a bond that lasted for the remainder of Reb Aharon's years. It was a bond with Reb Aharon, with the Rebbetzin, with Reb Shneur, and with all of Reb Aharon's family, and it continued as long as my father was alive.

Rebbetzin Chana Perel Kotler would call my father for Brachos. After Reb Aharon's passing, I once accompanied him to a Kotler family simcha in Brooklyn, where he stopped in for a short time to wish Mazel Tov. The Rebbetzin and her daughter Rebbetzin Soroh were effusive in their thanks to him for coming. "What a Kavod it is for us. What a Kavod!" Rebbetzin Chana Perel exclaimed over and over.

Tzidkus Stands Forever

After I came to Lakewood, Reb Aharon would give me an esrog to give to my father before Succos. In those days, finding an esrog that was surely not murkov was a difficult thing. I remember one time that Reb Aharon said to me, "And tell him that it is vaday not murkov," and he smiled broadly.

Twice, I have heard from others that Reb Aharon, sitting in his place on the mizrach, had seen my father entering at the other end of the Beis Medrash and risen to his feet. Those who told me this also added that my father never again entered the Beis Medrash when Reb Aharon was there. This story is believable on the part of both of them, surely on my father's part. But I knew that those relating the story had not actually seen it firsthand. However, recently I was recently told by Rav Chaim Bressler, Rosh Yeshiva of the Yeshiva of Scranton, that at the Bar Mitzvah celebration of Rav Yaakov Eliezer Schwartzman, Reb Aharon's oldest grandchild, my father entered and Reb Aharon upon seeing him rose to his feet. Rav Bressler also added, that when Reb Aharon stood up, of course all those assembled rose with him. I was also present at that time, and though I remember certain other details of that bar mitzvah, I have no memory of this incident. I assume that this is because I knew of their relationship and therefore didn't consider Reb Aharon's response in any way surprising.

Before I came to Lakewood, my father used to call Reb Aharon on a very frequent basis. After I came to

Tzidkus Stands Forever

Lakewood, my father began calling me and asking me to go into Reb Aharon and ask him questions on his behalf. I would do so and then call my father back with an answer, but I didn't understand why he didn't just call Reb Aharon himself directly.

Only years later did I understand. And once when sending a young man to Lakewood I told him to do everything he could to speak frequently with Reb Shneur. I always encourage youngsters to speak as often as possible with the Roshei Yeshivos of the various yeshivas they attend.

I know of two other incidents which occurred in the late 1930s. These are incidents which my father would consider not worthy of mention, but which son does. The first was told to me by someone who had been part of the group. A certain nasty man who had a store on Rockaway Boulevard required a blood transfusion. In those days transfusions were made from the donor to the recipient. My

Tzidkus Stands Forever

father recruited a group of store keepers who closed their stores and went in a group to the hospital to donate blood for him. After they completed their donations, my father said to them, "Come, let us go up to his room to wish him a Refuah Shelamah." They went upstairs and my father said to the sick man, "You see, all of these people came here to give blood for you." No doubt my father wanted to awaken some gratitude in the sick man. Instead, however, he growled curses at them and told them to get out of his room. "I would never have gone to the hospital to help that guy," my informant told me. "We only did it because of your father." The second incident which my father would not consider worthy of recording was something told to me by Reb Asher Zalke Rand, father of Rav Leibel Rand, who is the Rosh Kollel of the Far Rockaway Community Kollel.

Reb Asher told me that Rav Meir Karelitz arrived in the United States in 1939, and Reb Asher served as his driver. Immediately upon his arrival, Rav Karelitz asked to be driven out to South Ozone Park so that he could meet Rav Menachem Perr.

"Who is this Rav Menachem Perr?" Reb Asher asked, "Is he a gvir whom you expect to get a donation from?"

"He's not a gvir, he is a tremendous Tzadik" Rav Karelitz answered, "and I want to meet him!"

This story was told by Reb Asher to his son Reb Leibel many times. And when I happened to meet them both

Tzidkus Stands Forever

in the street on Chol Hamoad Pesach, Reb Asher told to it me also. How Rav Karelitz could have known about my father is truly amazing. But as I recount this incident, I see my father in my minds' eye, dismissing it with a motion of his hand, saying, "Alright Yechiel, alright."

In a letter my father wrote in the late 1930s to his cousin Leibel in Atlanta, Georgia, he expresses great contentment with his lot. "I have a good wife," he writes, "and three fine children. It would be nice if there was a little more parnosa, but all is well, B.H." My father and Leibel cherished their relationship, and Leibel saved all of my father's letters. In another undated letter, my father expresses great apprehension for their loved ones in Drohichin, as the ominous foreshadow of the oncoming war cast its pall upon the world. My father was active in trying to bring refugees to America. It was impossible for a refugee to be allowed in, even under the quota, without someone who would guarantee to support the immigrant, so that he would not fall on the welfare system for support. My father

Tzidkus Stands Forever

convinced a number of people to be guarantors, and was responsible for bringing over a number of refugees.

In an Agudath Israel publication "Orthodox Youth" of February 1941, there appeared the following item: "Rabbi Perr of Ozone Park should be especially mentioned for all his fine work on behalf of our Immigration Division." During the early days of the war, a refugee from Germany, Mrs. Loeb, worked in our home, helping my mother with the children and the housework. I suspect that my father had something to do with her immigrant status. I also discovered not long ago that my father was instrumental in bringing over a family named Weiss. In gratitude, they gave my parents a beautiful antique esrog box. He was also part of the group that helped in the escape of those Gedolim who reached these shores. Despite my father hiding from the limelight, in the book "Thy Brothers Blood," by David Kranzler, as well as in the book "Williamsburg Memories," by Gershon Kranzler, he is credited with having compiled the names of prominent Gedolim for rescue. Surely he was the qualified member of the group for this task.

But my father did much more than just compile lists of names. On Tuesday, Parshas Re'eh, August 27th 1940, Yisochor Behrend Strauss wrote a letter from Vichy France to his Rebbi, Rav Aharon Kotler. In the letter, written in a beautiful and learned Hebrew, he pleaded with Rav Aharon to help him to safety. Before Rosh Hashana of that year, he

Tzidkus Stands Forever

also sent Rav Aharon a telegram saying that he was in great danger and needed help immediately.

Rav Aharon had arrived in New York in the spring of 1940. He was deeply involved in Vaad Hatzalah and in rescuing his talmidim. Between Rosh Hashanah and Yom Kippur of that year, he forwarded Strauss's letter to my father.

In a cover letter, Rav Aharon addressed my father as Yedid Nafshi – my dear friend, and Kabir pe'ulos laTorah – a person of powerful deeds for Torah. He also wrote that he was sure that my father would take care of this matter with his usual alacrity.

On October 4, 1940, the day after Rosh Hashanah, a decree was issued in Vichy France to incarcerate all foreign Jews in internment camps. Strauss was a foreign Jew. He was from Antwerp.

The fact that Rav Aharon turned to my father in this matter, and also sent him the original letter from Strauss, is instructive. What occurred after my father received the letter, we do not know. But we do know that Rav Yisochor Behrend Strauss davened and learned regularly at the Lakewood minyan in Boro Park, for decades.

Tzidkus Stands Forever

A different effort by my father did not end successfully.

Rav Alexander Sender Vigodsky was a very close and dear friend of my father. They were about the same age. Both had learned in Slabodka, and previously in Maltch.

Rav Vigodsky was a major talmid chochom. He was the Rov of Beresa, a city not far from Drohichin. He had also learned Hora'ah under the tutelage of the Tzadik and Gaon Rav Simcha Zelig Reguer, who was the well-known Dayan of Brisk.

A number of warm letters from Rav Vigodsky to my father have been found, one of them dating back to as early as 1924. There are also some postcards. But there is also one postcard that is found much earlier. It is written in 1940, and it predates the others. In it Rav Vigodsky writes he received my father's telegram, for which he's very grateful, and that he would write to Moscow that very day. He also asked my father to write a detailed letter and also to contact the Russian Consulate in New York in order to make an effort on his behalf.

Tzidkus Stands Forever

Getting out of Russia was not the same as getting out of Vichy France. For a citizen of Russia it was impossible and Rav Vigodsky had been born in Kobryn. The government simply never responded to requests for exit permits.

On the other postcards postcards dated between December 31st, 1940 and May 25th, 1941 Rav Vigodsky repeatedly mentions the lack of news from his "relatives" in America and in Moscow. He also thanks my father for sending him packages. These were packages of dry goods that the recipients would sell in exchange for food.

Rav Vigodsky had a 20-year-old son, Yisroel, who was in Kovno, perhaps in the Slabodka Yeshiva. Rav Vigodsky thanked my father in a postcard, for the help his son had received through my father's relatives.

On February 26th, 1941 a telegram was received by my father from Kovno sent by Yisroel Vigodsky. In it he asked my father to send affidavits, to Moscow and to arrange an attestation of ship tickets, as demanded by the Japanese consul. Of course, this was a desperate attempt to leave Russia. He hoped that if he had an affidavit to America, and a transit visa from the Japanese consul, he might be given an exit permit from Moscow. It was about the results of such efforts that his father was asking, when he wrote of the lack of news from "his relatives" in America.

Tzidkus Stands Forever

On June 22nd, 1941 Germany attacked Russia. In 1942 Rav Vigodsky was among tens of thousands of Jews who were murdered.

After my father passed away, I was going through his things, and I came across a black leather wallet with a zipper all the way around. It was the type of wallet which was much favored by my friends when I was young. I had bought that wallet as a gift for my father in 1947. It was something that I, as a youngster, was sure he needed. As I unzipped it now, so many years later, I remembered my gratification, on those occasions over the years, when I would hear my father call out to my mother, "Lilly, maybe you saw my wallet?"

The wallet was now empty, except for the identification card with my father's name and address written in my own childish handwriting. I was about the put the empty wallet back in the drawer when I noticed what seemed to be a sliver of light brown wood crammed tightly into a corner of the wallet. I extricated it carefully and found that it was that post card which had been mailed to my father on December 16th 1940.. That card was written before the other postcards. It was found many years before the others. When I found the card, I did not know at all who the writer was, nor anything about the deep connection between my father and Rav Vigodsky.

The postcard had been written in 1940. I had given the wallet to my father seven years later in 1947. I was twelve at the time. Around that time, Jews in America were

Tzidkus Stands Forever

finding out what had occurred in Europe. When my father received the wallet, he hunted up that postcard and saved it in such a peculiar way, folding it tightly into a small square, and cramming into a corner of his wallet, so that it stayed there. I believe that my father, unable to help his friend escape the painful death which was finally inflicted upon him, kept that card in a safe way in his wallet, because of his pain at the loss of his friend, and because of his agmas nefesh that he was unable to save him.

Sunday morning, December 7, 1941, remains very clear in my memory. I remember hearing the news on the radio of the Japanese bombing of Pearl Harbor and running breathlessly down the street to tell my father. He was coming back from shul, and as I ran towards him I called out, "Daddy, Daddy, the Japanese have bombed Pearl Harbor! There's a war! There's a war!"

The seriousness of war struck me even as a child. I also remember how thrilled I and my younger siblings were when my father was somehow appointed as an air raid

Tzidkus Stands Forever

warden. He was issued an armband and a special helmet with which we would play. At the time of his appointment, my father was interviewed by some official who asked him what other occupation he was qualified to fill, if it became necessary for the war effort. My father answered that he could be a farmer. My mother, listening from the kitchen, greeted this idea with gales of laughter. She was seriously committed to caring for the vegetables in her "victory garden" in the back of the house. "What do you know about farming?" she asked him later. "Why not?" My father answered her, a little bit miffed. "It's no big Torah." No doubt farmers were not held in high esteem in Drohichin. As time went on, almost every Jewish young man in the community was drafted, and my father was deeply concerned that they should retain whatever connection to yiddishkeit they might have. He therefore collected all their addresses, and started sending them packages for Pesach. I remember that he obtained small, corrugated cardboard boxes, and sent each of them a box of matzos, salami, and a can of Pesach macaroons. I was drafted to help with assembling the boxes, and packing them, and addressing and gluing on the labels. I don't know how many such packages were sent out, but it was a large number, at least around a hundred. My father raised money for the project, and collected names of other Jewish boys as well. Those who contributed were not necessarily interested in preserving the Yiddishkeit of the boys, as they were in "doing something" for the boys. Eventually, this became a project of the National Council of Young Israel. I'm sure that my father must have

Tzidkus Stands Forever

given the idea to his friend Irving Bunim. I know of other projects, as well, in which my father enlisted others to spearhead the efforts. If I hadn't been told by those who led the project, no one would ever know of my father's involvement. In response to these packages, my father received grateful letters from the soldiers. These letters expressed the gratitude of terribly lonely men, who felt so cared for in those faraway places. Many times, these letters opened the door for a response, and my parents did their best to respond. These letters arrived in miniature photographic format that was called V-Mail. I saved them and over time I had a huge collection of those V-Mail letters.

Erev Succos was the last day of a short shiva for my father. Around three in the afternoon, Rav Avrohom Aharon Malinowitz arrived. He was out of breath and he was worried. He had come from a very long train ride from the Lower East Side, and then he had walked rapidly from the Far Rockaway station to my home. His first words were "I was afraid that you had already gotten up from shiva."

Tzidkus Stands Forever

Rav Malinowitz went on to explain that when he was in Shanghai during the war, the very first packages to arrive were from a Rabbi Perr in South Ozone Park. He was so deeply moved that in this far away and alien place, another yid, who didn't know them, had reached out to them to help, that he never forgot the kindness. He came to the shiva to express his thankfulness.

Shortly after the war ended and the men came back home, a motion was raised at a shul meeting not to renew the Rabbi's contract. Despite my father's sterling midos tovos, there were a few members who complained that "the Rabbi is too religious for us." I never heard a word about this from my father, but my mother was very upset, and it was she who told me. Of course, I was very nervous about the outcome.

I remember very vividly my mother's triumphant look on the morning after that important meeting. The word about the meeting had gotten out in town, and the week before the meeting, a large number of the veterans to whom

Tzidkus Stands Forever

my father had sent packages became members of the shul. That meeting was packed, with a turnout never before seen in the shul. At the meeting, when the agenda came to the report of the committee that was to look into my father's future, one of the veterans stood up and demanded to know exactly who the people were who had appointed this committee. At this point, there was an outburst of anger around the room, and the whole motion was dropped. This I know from my mother. No doubt my father would have been very upset that she had told me. Some of his baalei batim actually revered him. Most of the others respected him deeply.

At a memorial for my father held in shul shortly after his passing, a woman stood up, uninvited, to say something. What she said was that the Rabbi had asked her husband to close his store on Shabbos and he answered that he couldn't. The Rabbi then asked him not to smoke on Shabbos, and "the rest of his life, he never smoked on Shabbos, out of respect for the Rabbi."

But of course while he was generally respected, there were also a few who were completely unreachable. I once heard a particularly nasty person chortling to a friend of his in the shul. "I got the Rabbi on a string!" he said. "Wad'ya mean?" the other asked. "Every once in a while he comes to my house and asks me to forgive him for something. I don't know what. And I tell him 'I don't forgive you!' and he comes

Tzidkus Stands Forever

back again." This he told with loud laughter, ignoring the fact that I was right there in the room at the time.

On the way home from shul, I asked my father about it. My father answered that once when this man's son was disrupting the little group of Talmud Torah students, my father told him to leave the room. And at the time, he snapped at him "I don't need you here, and I don't need your father here! 'I don't need you here,' I had a right to say," my father explained, "but 'I don't need your father' was wrong for me to say. So I go to him to ask him for mechila."

"Dad," I asked, "Was this guy in the room at the time?"

"Of course not," my father answered, "but there were children in the room, and I said it in front of them."

"But Dad!" I protested, "They are only eight year olds!"

"And if they're only eight years old- so what?" My father asked, "I was mevayesh him in front of them!"

I then told my father that this man was mocking his asking mechila. He was silent for a moment. "Nu," he shrugged, "if so- I'll stop asking him." Of course my father understood this person's character, and that his Tzidkus was being used against him. But this didn't matter to him. What mattered to him was that he be cleansed from what he

Tzidkus Stands Forever

perceived to be a sin. For this he was willing for this person to toy with him.

Sometime around that same time, my father was approached with the offer of the Rabbonus of one of the largest shuls in Boro Park. Although Boro Park was not at that time what it is today, it was nevertheless a tempting offer. I was, of course, a child, but my father tried out the idea on me. "Daddy," I said to him, "have you made all the Jews in South Ozone Park frum?" That answer may have been enough to sway my father in the direction of staying where he was. I know I was not responsible, but I've always felt bad about giving him that answer.

The truth is however, that it was because of his great sense of responsibility that he chose to remain in South Ozone Park. My father felt a profound responsibility to his community. His feeling of responsibility was such that he was never away from shul on a Shabbos. There was only one Shabbos that he went away, and that was to attend the Bar Mitzvah of one of his grandsons, Yonoson Tendler, in Baltimore. "I have not been away from the shul on a Shabbos in forty years," he confided to Rav Shlomo Teitelbaum shortly before that Shabbos, "and it hurts my heart to do so. But what can I do? My wife insists!"

"Forty years and not to leave once!" Rav Shlomo repeated to me with wonder. "Forty years!"

Tzidkus Stands Forever

It seems that it was in the early 1940s that my father started to learn bechavrusa with Rav Chinitz, one of Roshei Yeshiva of Torah Vodaath. This chavrusa continued for over 40 years. They learned together in person and over the telephone. As far as I know, learning on the telephone was my father's chidush. I remember the surprise of some of my father's friends when they heard about this. But thinking for himself, and coming up with new solutions to problems, was something that was typical of my father. My father, of course, was very close with Rav Chinitz and took me to visit him once in the apartment where he lived alone, and a second time later still, when he was in a nursing home. My father had many face-to-face chavrusas. Rav Simcha Wasserman told me that he learned bechavrusa for two years with my father, around 1940. They learned Masechta Avoda Zara. My father had also many other Chavrusas, of whom I only know a few. He learned with Rav Moshe Avraham Greenspan, with Rav Grainom Lezevnik, and with Rav Dovid Teitz from Brooklyn for a great number of years. I've recently been told that he had a mishnayos seder with Rabbi Shmaryahu Shulman and learned Masechta Shabbos with Rav Shlomo Teitelbaum. He also learned with the Naroler Rebbe, Rav Shapiro. I've been told that they completed many masechtos together. I had the pleasure of meeting the Rebbe and he spoke highly of my father, raising his hands up as he spoke. I frequently meet his son, the present Rebbe, Reb Beirish, who is especially warm to me because of the past connection. For several decades, my father learned every day with a Chavrusa downstairs in the

Tzidkus Stands Forever

Bais Hatalmud, which was then located in East New York. During that time, he became close with the great talmidei chochamim there and with Rav Leib Malin.

Someone described to me a scene at the Bais Hatalmud. My father had been given an aliya and noticed that the stitches attaching two sections of the sefer Torah were torn. He called out to Reb Leib and asked him if he should make the brocho. Reb Leib called back to him from his place that he will not paskin, and that my father should decide himself. My father stood at the Torah and kept repeating, "Nu, Reb Leib, should I make a brocho?" I was never told the conclusion of the story. The witness only shared this scene, which he said was engraved in his memory.

Tzidkus Stands Forever

Not long ago, a long-forgotten experience came back to me. Someone was asking me about the Kashrus of a certain restaurant, when I suddenly remembered being about seven years old and standing on Sutphin Boulevard in Jamaica with my father, waiting for the Q9 bus that would take us back home. A short distance away at the corner stood a hotdog vendor with one of those carts which have a large umbrella over it.

My father was pacing back and forth, deep in thought, and casting glances from time to time in the direction of the vendor. Finally, he made a decision. "Come, Yechiel," he said to me. He took my hand and led me over to the vendor. "I would like to buy a frankfurter for my son," he said. I was very confused. My parents permitted me to eat only in my own home, and here my father was buying me a hot dog! Didn't he know that these hot dogs weren't kosher?

The vendor opened the steamer, started taking out a frankfurter, paused, and then said, as far as I remember in Yiddish, "Ober Rebbe, es is nisht kosher! – but Rabbi, it is not kosher!"

"Nisht kosher!" my father said, feigning surprise. "I thought when I saw a yiddishe mentch like you selling frankfurters, that surely they were kosher. How does it come that you sell nisht kosher?"

I paid no attention to the rest of the conversation, but when the memory of this incident came back to me I

Tzidkus Stands Forever

began to laugh. It was so typical of my father! It was typical of my father to call the attention of perfect strangers to Torah observance.

I remember traveling with him in a taxi as a teenager. My father only rarely traveled by taxi, but it was erev Shabbos, and in order to be home in time for Shabbos, we had taken a taxi. "Can you see the driver's name?" my father asked me in a whisper, motioning with his head to the driver's permit, which was displayed behind a foggy little plastic window on my side of the taxi. I leaned forward and made out the name next to the photograph displayed in the little lighted window. "Levine," I whispered back. "Mr. Levine," my father called out from the back seat, "are you sure that you will be able to return your taxi to the garage in enough time to be home for Shabbos?"

Mr. Levine was silent for a while, and then he said, "Well, I'll tell you the truth Rabbi, I don't keep Shabbos!"

"You don't keep Shabbos?" my father asked, "How is it possible that a Jew doesn't keep Shabbos?"

This time Mr. Levine answered with quite a bit of indignation, "Come on Rabbi, how many Jews keep Shabbos?"

As the conversation continued, I remember him becoming more and more angry. My father, however, was not to be deterred, nor was he apologetic. He continued his appeal very calmly. I don't remember the outcome. Surely my father did not succeed with Mr. Levine. But on such

Tzidkus Stands Forever

occasions, he would usually ask that the person to do just one thing for Shabbos: not to smoke on Shabbos, or not to write on Shabbos, or to unscrew the bulb in their refrigerator at home before Shabbos.

Of all the many thousands of times that my father asked Jews to keep Shabbos, or at least some part of Shabbos, he did succeed a number of times. In at least one case that I know of he was very successful. I found out about this success when we were sitting shiva for my father. At the shiva, there was a gentleman who sat patiently for quite a long time, waiting to tell me his story. "My name is Kavon," he finally introduced himself, "and I have a store," and he went on to give the location, which was several miles from my parents' home. "Thirteen years ago," he , "I got a phone call from your father. He said to me, 'Mr. Kavon, this year Rosh Hashanah comes out on Shabbos. Maybe because it is also Rosh Hashanah you'll close your store for this Shabbos?'

"I said to him, 'Rabbi, twenty nine years my store is open on Shabbos and no one ever told me once to close it. I've got cousins who are Rabbis, and not once did any of them say to me to close for Shabbos! And you asked me to close for Shabbos! Rabbi, I promise you, I will not only close the store for this Shabbos, but I will close it for every Shabbos from now on. 29 years I was open on Shabbos! It's enough already!' "These last thirteen years have been the happiest in my life," Mr. Kavon continued, wiping his eyes. "I

Tzidkus Stands Forever

go to shul every Shabbos and Yom Tov and I'm even the Gabbai for Krias HaTorah; and I'm very very happy."

"Tell me," I asked Mr. Kavon, "had my father ever spoken to you before that phone call about Shabbos? Did you know him from before?"

"Well, of course I'd heard of Rabbi Perr," he said. "But I had never spoken to him. I didn't know him at all."

Louis Bertenthal had a Liquor store on Rockaway Boulevard, near 132nd street. I was sent there many times to buy a bottle of wine for Kiddush.

I remember one time when I brought the bottle over to Mr. Bertenthal at the cash register, that he suddenly seized the bottle and put it under the counter. I asked him later why he had done so, and he explained that a gentile had just entered the store, and he hid the bottle so that the gentile would not see the wine.

Tzidkus Stands Forever

This seemed very strange to me, especially since he the wines were displayed openly on shelves, all around the store, and most of his customers were gentiles.

Later, I asked my father about this, and he told me that this custom, that a gentile should not even see the wine, is brought in the sefer, Shaloh.

Some years later, Mr. Bertenthal passed away and my father attended his funeral. I heard from someone that my father had spoken very strongly at the funeral, and I was surprised. It wasn't like him, and I asked him about it.

"What should I tell you, Yechiel?" my father said, "The first speaker was from the Masonic Temple where Mr. Bertenthal had been a member. He painted a beautiful picture of the wonderful world that the deceased was going to, denying that there is any Judgement at all. I felt *mechuyav* to say that he will now be brought before divine Judgment and asked why his store was open on Shabbos, why he didn't keep Kosher, and all the other *Mitzvos* of the *Torah*. I couldn't sit there in silence and allow all the people to listen to *Apikorsus*."

Tzidkus Stands Forever

A visit to my Bobeh in Coney Island was a long, seemingly endless trip from South Ozone Park, by bus and then by subway. When my father took me along, we usually reviewed mishnayos on the trip. "Uvelechtecha Baderech" my father would call it. Sometime around 1946, we were coming back from a visit to Coney Island, when a passenger got on the train at one of the stations, carrying a fishing rod and some other paraphernalia. He sat down across the aisle from us and put a small cardboard box on the seat in front of him. The train moved on, and I paid no attention until I realized that the fisherman had gotten off, leaving the small cardboard box behind on the seat. I got up and took the box, and found that it contained an expensive looking fishing reel. I had learned Bava Metzia with my father, and my father analyzed with me what we should do with the reel. He then said that although I was permitted to keep the reel, since it was left in an unguarded place, I should still turn it in to the Lost and Found, because maybe its owner will seek it, and returning it to him might bring about a Kiddush Hashem.

We got off the train at Sutphin Boulevard, and I turned in the reel to the agent in the change booth there. I told him that if it was not claimed, I wanted it back. He wrote down my name and address, and told me that if the reel was not claimed in 90 days, I would get it back. Three months is a long time for a youngster to wait, especially when waiting for something so exciting. Those endless three months finally passed, and then another few days, and I began to nag my

Tzidkus Stands Forever

father to find out what happened, and maybe get the reel back for me. My father got on the phone and spoke to someone at the Transit Authority. Then, after another wait, a letter arrived which said that there was no record of a fishing reel being turned in, but upon investigation, a notation of my name and address was found in the change booth at the Sutphin Boulevard station. I should therefore come to the Lexington Avenue Extension, where an auction of unclaimed property was being prepared, and upon showing this letter to the person in charge, I would be permitted to choose for myself any fishing reel I wished.

If my nagging had brought me this far, it wasn't going to stop now. So shortly afterwards, my father and I were on the train to Lexington Avenue. There, we entered an extremely large underground room filled with the most surprising things that had been lost somewhere in the transit system during the past year. There seemed to be thousands of umbrellas, stacked almost to the ceiling along one long wall. There were cartons of eyeglasses, cartons of books, bales of garments, a box of dentures, even a new car tire – and a small box of fishing reels, over which I hovered, making up my mind which to choose. As I stood there deciding, one of the workers called my father down to the other side of the large room, saying, "Rabbi, here's something that you will be interested in!" I followed my father, and we were shown a large brown paper package, which was then opened to reveal a Sefer Torah. The Torah was without its atzei chaim and was rolled from Devarim to Bereishis. As I remember it, it had

Tzidkus Stands Forever

been wrapped in a worn velvet shulchan cover, over which the brown paper had then been wrapped. We were astonished and speechless.

When the shock passed, my father asked what would be done with the Torah, and he was told that it would be auctioned off to the highest bidder, just like everything else. My father asked when the auction would be held, and was given the date. It was a Saturday. My fishing reel paled into insignificance.

On the train ride home, I kept coming up with schemes for saving that Sefer Torah. I remember that we were coming down the staircase from the El at Lefferts Boulevard. when I accepted the fact that there was just no way we could do it. We came home, and my father got back on the phone with the Transit Authority. This time, he was speaking to people whom he had spoken to before, and he knew whom to ask for. He explained that a Sefer Torah is the most sacred object to Jews; and he requested that although he was unable because of the Sabbath to bid on it himself, the Transit Authority should be careful to auction it only to someone who would treat it with the proper respect. They answered that they would take the matter under consideration.

A few days later a letter arrived from the Transit Authority saying that they didn't know how to treat the Torah with proper respect, and therefore they asked that my

Tzidkus Stands Forever

father come down to the Lexington Avenue Extension and take possession of the Torah himself.

Shortly after we brought home the Torah, my father said to me that now that there was a Torah in the house, even a Torah that is posul, we all have to try to behave in a more careful manner. The staircase in our home in South Ozone Park came down directly into our dining room. Against the wall directly opposite the bottom of the stairs stood a tall bookcase, hammered together by some carpenter, which had once been painted some pinkish color. The bookcase was filled with my father's seforim, and it overflowed with his papers. My mother had assured all of us children on numerous occasions that my father's papers were "the bane of her existence." Up on top on the left side of the bookcase, wrapped in brown paper, the Sefer Torah lay for more than ten years.

Then, on one of my all too infrequent visits to my parents, I noticed that the brown package was gone. "What happened to the Sefer Torah?" I asked my father.

There was a pause. Then he answered, a little defensively, I thought, "I returned it."

"You returned it?" I said. "How did you find the person who lost it?"

"Well," he said, "when I used to meet a sofer, or when I went into a seforim store, I would ask if they ever heard of somebody who had lost a Sefer Torah.

Tzidkus Stands Forever

Not long ago I received a phone call from someone who heard that I was asking about someone who lost a Sefer Torah. He told me that he had once lost a Sefer Torah on the train. He was a refugee, and worked by day as a cutter in a factory. At night, he worked as a sofer to make a few extra dollars. He had been given a Torah to repair, and had removed the atzei chaim, as is usually done by sofrim, and took it home with him on the train.

Being very tired, he dozed off, and then woke up with a start as he realized he was at his station. He jumped up and quickly and got off, and only as the train pulled away did he remember the Sefer Torah. He was a newcomer in this country, and so he didn't know that he should inquire at the Lost and Found office. The sofer finally negotiated a settlement with the shul, and over a long period of time he paid them 3,000 dollars, which was a fortune in those days. If he would be given the Sefer Torah, he said he would get his money back from the shul. My father asked him for a certified check of 1,500 dollars, as a security, in case someone else would come with a claim, and then gave away the Torah to him.

"Dad," I said to my father, "you know that that was your Sefer Torah; it belonged to you, not to him. And I suppose," I couldn't resist adding, "that he gave you a siman that the first word is Bereishis."

"I know, I know," my father said, "but tell me Yechiel, lifnim mishuras hadin is nothing – just nothing?"

Tzidkus Stands Forever

It was either in 1946 or 1947 that my father told me what had occurred with him 10 years before. Right next to the shul was the meeting hall of the Wilbur E. Collier Post of the Veterans of Foreign Wars. The veterans were good neighbors with the shul, and they presented the shul with a flag pole and an American flag. They had the most profound respect for my father. Memorial Day at the end of May used to be an important and solemn occasion. It was marked by a very long parade of veterans and other uniformed groups down Rockaway Boulevard. The parade ended at a grandstand in Baisley Park, where speeches were given and rifles fired in a salute of honor to America's fallen soldiers.

My father was invited every year to offer the closing prayer, and during those years when I learned together with him at home, he once took me along with him on Memorial Day. My parents neither owned a car, nor did they know how to drive. My father and I started walking to Baisley Park along 116th Avenue. As we walked, we reviewed Mishnayos by heart, and we played his game of trying to think of Torah things that came in groups of numbers, all the two's and then all the three's and so on. It was a beautiful spring day, and we were strolling along when I said to my father, "We had better walk faster, or you'll be late."

"No," my father replied, "I want to be late."

"You want to be late?" I asked him. I was surprised, because my father was never late for anything.

Tzidkus Stands Forever

"You see," he said, "when I first came to town and they invited me to participate, I thought that I was the only clergyman on the program. I did not realize that I would make the closing prayer, but that a galach was invited to make the opening prayer. I came on time, they put me up on the bimah in the front row, and the galach got up and said, 'Please rise'. Everybody stood up except for me. Then he said, 'Uncover,' and everyone removed their hats except for me. I sat there in the front of everyone with my tall yarmulka on. There were maybe several thousand people there, and every eye was staring only at me. It was the most difficult moment of my life. Since then I'm careful to come late."

After I recuperated a little from this story I asked him, "Dad, isn't there any heter to stand up?"

He said to me, "To stand up in honor of avodah zorah — chalila! It is yehoreig v'ahl yaavor!"

My father's story had a profound impact on me. I had my first opportunity not to stand up "in honor of avodah zorah, chalila," on a bus not long afterwards, when a nun, dressed in old fashioned full habit, got on the bus and stood herself in the aisle right next to where I was sitting wearing my yarmulka. I had been trained by my father to always give my seat to a woman or an older man who was standing. However, this woman was a nun. My standing up for her might be considered "in honor of avodah zorah, chalila." On the other hand, it was not unusual then for men in those times to give their seats to women: To not do so was seen as

Tzidkus Stands Forever

lacking in my manners. "Sofek D'Oraiso L'Hachmir" was my decision, and I spent the rest of the trip sitting very uncomfortably under what seemed to me to be the angry gaze of the nun. The experience helped me appreciate what my father went through on that Memorial Day. A few years ago, there was a dedication scheduled for the Jewish Chapel in the local hospital in Far Rockaway. I was away for Shabbos, and Rav Aaron Brafman, the menahel of Yeshiva called me to say that a local Rabbi was afraid that there would only be a small Jewish turnout. He had asked the Yeshiva to send bochurim to enlarge the attendance at the dedication. I said to Rav Brafman, "There will surely be a galach there, and he will offer a prayer, and everyone will stand up in honor of avodah zora, chalila. It is yehoreig v'ahl yaavor! We can't go!" And that is exactly what happened at the dedication.

Tzidkus Stands Forever

In the late forties, the house next to ours on 130th Street was bought by a gentile family who had a bratty young daughter named Florinda. Not long after they bought the house, they demolished the rickety fence that had separated our two back yards and began replacing it with a new picket fence. As the new supporting posts were being put into the ground, I noticed that the new fence wandered about a foot over into our backyard. I knew that there was no use complaining about it to my father, so my brother and I undertook a campaign of "psychological warfare" against Florinda's family. Every day we used to cut through the back yard, and then the empty lot behind it, to get to our bus stop to go to Yeshiva. From then on, my brother and I would pause every time we went along the fence, and then conspicuously bend over and sight along it, so that Florinda's father would know that we were fully aware of what he was doing. Within a short time, our "psychological warfare" had an effect, but not the effect we had planned.

A few days had passed when Florinda's father saw me in the back yard and called me over. "Son," he said to me, "let me tell you a story. There were once two men who had an argument about a piece of land. This one said, 'It belongs to me,' and the other said, 'It belongs to me.' So they both went to a judge, and the judge thought about it and then said, 'You're both wrong, the land doesn't belong to either of you. You both belong to the land!' You get it son?" he asked, "the judge was saying, 'what's the point in fighting over a piece of

Tzidkus Stands Forever

land, you're both gonna die anyway.' You get it son? D'ya get it?"

"I get it. I get it," I answered, while I wondered at the nerve of this crook to tell me such a story.

"You know," Florinda's father said proudly "that's a story from the Talmud!"

"From the Talmud!" I said astonished, "How come you know it?"

"Yes," he repeated "it's from the Talmud. Your father told me that story."

It must have been during the summer of 1949. Yeshiva was over for the year. Some of my classmates went off to Camp Morris; many did not. I didn't, because I was allergic to summer grasses. I didn't feel well up in the mountains.

I was sitting on the stoop of our house one early afternoon when a seedy looking man walked down the street

Tzidkus Stands Forever

and asked for my father. I told him that my father should be home shortly, and said that if he wished he could sit down on the stoop with me and wait. This person was clearly in bad shape. His clothes were worn and filthy. He smelled from perspiration on this hot day. He was clearly here seeking tzedaka. We sat together for a few minutes and then I saw my father coming down the street. I went to meet him and told him that this person with me was waiting for him. My father greeted the man with sholom aleichem and invited him into the house. I also went in, went upstairs to my room, and started reading a book. A few minutes later, I heard my father's footsteps coming up the stairs. From his slow and deliberate pace, I knew that he was engrossed in thought, and I suspected that I was in trouble. A moment later, he tapped on the bedroom door and came in.

"Tell me, Yechiel," he asked, "why didn't you invite the man into the house?"

"It's very hot in the house, I thought that outside there is at least a breeze."

It was true that we had no air conditioning, and it was cooler outside. But this wasn't the whole truth. I also found this person repellent, and this was the main reason for not inviting him in. Of course, I knew that I better not say this to my father.

"Oh," my father said, "it is very hot! Tell me Yechiel, if it's so hot, did you offer this man a glass of cold water?

Tzidkus Stands Forever

"No, I didn't," I admitted reluctantly. "I didn't think of it."

This excuse sounded lame even to me, but I was still not willing to admit I was wrong. My father was looking at me and thinking about what to say next. After a minute he said, "Tell me Yechiel, how do you know this man is not Eliyahu Hanavi who came here to test your hachnosas orchim?"

"C'mon, dad," I said with exasperation, "you know that he's not Eliyahu Hanavi!"

"No, no, I really mean it," my father insisted. "How do you know that he's not Eliyahu Hanavi? How do you know! Tell me!"

"Well, for one thing - he doesn't have a beard!" I said, sure that I had settled the question once and for all.

"So tell me now Yechiel," my father said, "how do you know that Eliyahu Hanavi has a beard?"

I don't remember my father ever speaking about Eliyahu Hanavi except for this one occasion. His remark about Eliyahu Hanavi possibly not having a beard shaped my own attitudes about frumkeit and tzidkus ever since. Since then, I can accept the possibility that Eliyahu Hanavi may not have a beard. Come to think of it, neither did my father.

Tzidkus Stands Forever

It was around 1950, and I was accompanying my father on one of his Friday afternoon walks on Rockaway Boulevard. My father would often take such a walk, and he would stop in at some of the stores to speak with the proprietors and remind them that Shabbos or Yom Tov was coming. Of course, just the fact that he stopped in was itself a reminder.

That afternoon, as we walked down Lincoln Street towards Rockaway Boulevard, we passed a line of people waiting at the Q9 bus stop. Waiting in line for the bus was a Jewish woman. My father stopped and greeted her. "Where are you going?" he asked her pleasantly. "Oh," she told him, "there is a big sale going on in Gertz's Department store in Jamaica. I'm going to see if they have some things that I need."

"But it is not very long until licht benchen," my father said. "It doesn't seem that you would be able to come back in time for Shabbos."

The woman began to hem and haw. "That's true," she said, "but I do need some things."

"But Shabbos is so much more important," my father said. "Why don't you just go home now, and you'll get those things another time?"

"Well," the woman said, "I couldn't just do that, because I promised my friend here that I'd go shopping with

Tzidkus Stands Forever

her." With this she indicated the gentile woman who was standing in line behind her.

"I will speak to your friend for you," my father volunteered, and at this, he was introduced to the gentile woman.

"Are you a Rabbi?" the woman asked. "I've never spoken to a Rabbi before. I am just so thrilled to meet you! You know," she continued, "a Rabbi was supposed to speak at my granddaughter's graduation from P.S. 155 this morning, but he couldn't come, and he sent the most beautiful telegram which they read at the graduation. But I don't know who that Rabbi is," she ended ruefully.

"I am the Rabbi," my father answered.

"You are!" the woman exclaimed. "Rabbi, I am so excited! It was the most beautiful message I ever heard!" It was indeed a beautiful telegram. I had seen my mother struggling over it early that morning. My father then went on to explain to the gentile women that since her friend was Jewish, she wouldn't be able to go shopping with her, because Jewish women must light candles before sunset, which would be very soon. Would she forgive her friend for not going with her? The gentile woman was most gracious about it, and the Jewish woman then apologized to her friend and made a rather reluctant departure.

Tzidkus Stands Forever

My father then turned right onto Rockaway Boulevard. As we passed P.S. 96, I heard my father begin to sigh very loudly.

"Are you alright?" I asked him, worried that perhaps he suddenly didn't feel well.

"Oy, I just did a terrible thing, a terrible thing. Didn't you see what I just did?" my father asked. "No," I said, "what did you do?"

"I said 'I am the Rabbi,'" my father answered.

"So what's wrong with that?" I asked. "You are the Rabbi!"

"Yechiel, I'm surprised at you," my father said. "Didn't we learn that Shmuel Hanavi was punished for saying 'Onochi Haroeh' - I am the Prophet. Because of that, he had no Ruach Hakodesh at Yishai's house! And I had to say 'I am the Rabbi'? Oy, why did I say that!" And he shook his head in regret. Young as I was, I understood him, and I understood his regret.

Tzidkus Stands Forever

It was shortly before Pesach in 1950 when my father took me along with him to Baisley Park. On Sutphin Boulevard, there was a shul that had once been Orthodox. As the community declined, they turned Conservative in the hope of attracting more members. Finally they became Reform, but that did not help either. Eventually, the shul closed, and the keys remained in the possession of a druggist whose store was located a few blocks from the shul. The druggist had given the keys away to a group of black people who were now using the shul. How my father knew this story, I did not ask, but it was his intention to speak to the druggist.

The druggist was unconcerned with what he had done. "They have a letter from the organization of Reform congregations that recognizes them as Jews," he claimed. "That's good enough for me."

"But they can't be Jews. They don't observe Shabbos. They don't observe the Torah," my father protested.

"Look, Rabbi," the druggist answered, "I don't observe the Torah either, and I'm still Jewish."

In vain, my father tried to explain the difference between being born Jewish and becoming Jewish. The druggist refused to understand. "And what happened with the Torahs?" my father asked. "We have two Torahs, and they are still in the shul," the druggist answered.

Tzidkus Stands Forever

We left the druggist, my father very much upset. At home, he remained much perturbed, and the family too picked up on his distress. My sister Esther had her room on the third floor, in what we called "the attic." My brother Eliezer and I shared the back bedroom. Early Shabbos morning, before davening, there was a knock on our door, and my sister came bounding into our room. "I have a terrific idea," she said, "but first you must promise me that you will not leave me out." The assurance was given, and Esther said, "Let's break into the shul and steal the Sifrei Torah!" The excitement that flowed through my body was like a sudden jolt of electricity. We instantly jumped up and started talking about how we could go about it. At the davening that morning, I took a certain youngster into our confidence. This youngster was a ben bayis in our home and ate the Shabbos meals with us. Today, he is Rav Chaim Bressler, the Rosh Yeshiva of the Yeshiva Gedolah of Scranton.

After the seudah, the four of us went for a "Shabbos walk." We walked to Baisley Park to "case the joint." When we arrived at the building, we saw that there was some sort of activity going on. Without much hesitation, we opened the door and entered the foyer of the shul. The foyer no longer looked like an entrance to a shul. On the wall facing us was a sign, which read, "Do not disturb the High Priestess before 10 am." We were met in the foyer by a well-dressed burly black gentleman wrapped in a talis, who refused us entry into the shul, saying that it was permitted only for members. To our questions, the gentleman explained that the congregants

Tzidkus Stands Forever

were not Jews at all; rather, they were Hebrews. They followed not the teachings of Moses, but of Melchizedek. When asked if they followed the commandments of the Torah, he responded that each congregant was a priest or a priestess, and each decided on his or her own what to do.

We then asked if they had the Torahs, to which he answered, "Yes." When asked why they needed them since they were the Laws of Moses not Melchizedek, our informant told us that they nevertheless wanted to keep them, because, "They're an original thing, know what I mean?" During this conversation, we could hear the congregants through the closed doors.

A woman, possibly the late-sleeping High Priestess, was rehearsing with the congregation. "Kosher lepesach," she would say, and they would respond in unison "Kosher lepesak." "Pesach, Pesach," she repeated, emphasizing the "ach" sound. "Ach, ach, ach," she said, and they repeated after her, trying to pronounce the sound.

Our excitement mounted during the Shabbos, and after havdalah we insisted to our skeptical mother that we had to go out again for a walk. We hunted up a little zippered canvas overnight bag, into which we put screwdrivers, pliers, a hammer, and one or two other tools that we thought might be useful. We also took two plastic raincoats in which to wrap the two Sifrei Torah, and then just the three of us set off again for Sutphin Boulevard.

Tzidkus Stands Forever

119-09 Sutphin Boulevard is a converted storefront, the fourth in a row of attached one-story buildings, stretching south from the intersection of 119th Avenue. To make the structure into a shul, a brick facade had been added which contained large double doors, flanked on either side by a small arched window. To distinguish it further from its storefront neighbors, a tall cupola was erected on the flat roof of the shul. Sutphin Boulevard is busy even at night, and across the intersection of 119th Avenue was an especially busy bar, with customers constantly going in and out. The first plan we had was to try to enter from behind the building, where it was dark. We went onto 119th Avenue and turned down the first driveway. That should have led us behind the shul. However, the gravel made an awfully loud sound as it crunched beneath our shoes. We removed our shoes and continued further, despite the pain in our feet from the gravel, when suddenly a dog started barking nearby very loudly. We beat a hasty retreat back to the street.

In order to be as inconspicuous as possible, we then started strolling up and down the block in front of the shul, while glancing at it furtively. In one of our passes, I saw that one of the little glasses in the upper half of the left front window was broken. We strolled to the corner and turned back. On the next pass, a fast look around showed that "the coast was clear," and I reached up and lifted the piece of glass out of its frame. We strolled to the corner, and I dropped the glass into the sewer. On the next pass, I reached into the now open window frame and turned the

Tzidkus Stands Forever

catch that kept the upper and lower windows locked into position. On the next pass, I tried to lift the bottom window, and saw that it would indeed open. We passed again in front of the building, and then checked that the street was again empty. I shoved up the window, crouched down against the wall, and my brother Eliezer climbed up over me and in through the window. Glancing down Sutphin Boulevard, I saw in the distance some traffic coming up the street. My brother's legs were sticking straight out from the open window. I pushed the bottoms of his shoes straight in, and pulled down the window. My sister and I strolled to the corner.

On the next several passes, when it was safe, we tried the handle on the front door, but it was still locked. What could have happened to my brother? Then, passing near the window we heard a "psst." My brother had fallen into a restroom that was out of order, and had been locked from the other side. He was unable to get out. When it was safe, our bag of tools was passed to him through the window, and we shut the window again. A few minutes later he jiggled the front door. We looked around, it was safe, and we went in.

As we quietly entered and passed through the foyer into the shul, we saw a doorway on the front left which led further on behind the Aron Kodesh. There was a light shining through this doorway into the shul. The first thing we had to know was if we were alone in the building. With racing hearts,

Tzidkus Stands Forever

we stealthily entered into that backroom, and found to our great relief that the light was on but there was no one there. The shul itself no longer looked like a shul. It had been altered by its new occupants. All that was left from the way a shul looks was the center of the Paroches, visible through a gap which had been left purposely open in the paneling which they had installed across the front of the room.

We reached through the opening in the paneling, and opened the Poroches and Aron Kodesh. Inside we found only one Sefer Torah. We took it out and wrapped it carefully in one of the raincoats we had brought with us. We also had to be careful about leaving the shul. There was no way of seeing from inside the building if the street was clear. Once again, my brother went first. He walked boldly out the door. As he did so, a taxi slowed and stopped for the red light at the intersection of 119th Ave. The driver's attention was caught by this white kid, unexpectedly emerging from a building in the middle of the night. They glanced at each other. My brother walked to the curb, cleared his throat loudly, spat into the street, and turned around and started back boldly toward the building. The light changed to green. The taxi drove off. The street was quiet. I wiped off the doorknobs, and we emerged into the street. We rapidly crossed over the well-lit Sutphin Boulevard and entered the safety of the darker side streets. My sister Esther was carrying the Torah. Before leaving the shul, she had said, "I want to carry the Torah. A girl never gets the chance to carry

Tzidkus Stands Forever

a Torah." She had the first chance to carry it on the way home.

I have participated in many Torah processions, but I have never since experienced the joy that we three felt that night, carrying home the Torah. We were singing quietly and dancing all the way. When we arrived home, we didn't want to risk smuggling it into the house, so we hid it in the garage.

My father was sitting in his usual place, with his Gemara, when we came in. My mother had gone to bed. "Where have you been?" he asked. "Oh, nothing. We just went for a long walk," I answered. "Did you have a fight with shkotzim?" my father asked, seeing how excited we were. We reassured him that this was not so. He shrugged, and ordered us off to bed.

We waited for a day when our parents were away, and we brought the Sefer Torah up to my sister's room, "the attic." We wrapped it up and placed it, deep and hidden, in the large attic closet in which my mother stored extra blankets and linens. The Sefer Torah remained there, untouched and unknown to my parents, for about six or seven years. For a while, at every opportunity, I would listen to the news. I was expecting to hear about the theft on the newscasts. I remember being even a little bit disappointed that it was never reported.

Tzidkus Stands Forever

With the passage of time, I stopped cringing when seeing a policeman. Yet I was bothered by my conscience; had I committed the aveira of geneiva?

About three years later, when I was a talmid at the Yeshiva of Philadelphia, I sat down with Rav Dov Schwartzman, who was one of the Roshei Yeshiva at the time, and I asked him my question. As I told him the story, with only some of the details, I saw Reb Dov starting to breathe faster. When I finished and came to my question, Reb Dov answered quickly, and passionately: "If you hadn't done it already, you'd be mechuyov to go do it now!"

"Well," I said to Reb Dov, "the second Sefer Torah may have been returned there by now, and they may also have seforim and mezuzos there to be saved!"

"No! No! No! No!" Reb Dov said, and held up his hands as if to stop me. "I don't mean that you should go in there again. I mean that what you did was right!"

A few years later still, I was in Lakewood. There I heard that P'eylim was asking for Sefrei Torah to be sent to communities in Eretz Yisroel. My sister and brother were in agreement that this would be a very good thing to do with the Sefer Torah. But I still wasn't sure about the geneiva problem. Reb Dov had been just a bit too enthusiastic in his agreement with what we had done. He might have been carried away by his enthusiasm. I went in to Rav Aharon Kotler. I told him the story more briefly than I had told it to

Tzidkus Stands Forever

Reb Dov. Reb Aharon answered, "They had no right to give it away. You had the right to take it. It is not stolen. It would be a good thing to give it to P'eylim." I called Rav Avrohom Hirsch from P'eylim and arranged for the Sefer Torah to be picked up in a few days. I needed the time to be able to tell my father.

I came home from Yeshiva and my father asked me to go somewhere with him. We started walking down 130th street, and I raised the subject. "Do you remember some years ago that all the kids were out very late on a Motzoei Shabbos?" He didn't. I went on to tell him what we had done. He stopped walking, and was quiet for a minute. Then he said, "Let's go back home, I want to see it."

We went back home and upstairs to the attic. I unwrapped the Torah, and he looked at it wordlessly for a while. Then he said, "Tell me, Yechiel, you weren't afraid of being arrested?" We were back in the street again when he told me, "When I came home from Slabodka, the Cossacks came into Drohichin and burned down the shuls. There were four shuls in Drohichin, and they burned all of them. There was a back way into the shul where we davened, and I went in while it burned, and saved a Sefer Torah. The Cossacks were all around. Had they seen me they would have shot me. I was meshugah to do such a thing. It was the only Sefer Torah to survive. The whole town came to our house to hear Krias Hatorah."

"How old were you at the time?" I asked.

Tzidkus Stands Forever

"I was around your age," he answered. Then he thought for a minute. "No, not your age," he said, "a little older; but around your age anyway."

𝕴n the early 1950s, the Korean War was waging, and a number of young men from the community were drafted into the army.

Howard Schwartz had been influenced by my father to be careful to eat only Kosher. When he was drafted, he came to my father and asked him, "What about Kosher?"

My father said to him, "When you're in war, and by not eating you will be weak, then you can eat whatever you want to keep yourself strong. But try not to eat something that could never have been Kosher," my father added.

Howard went on to become an officer, and he was awarded a bronze star for bravery.

Tzidkus Stands Forever

"When I was in training in Texas," Howard said, "I ate only vegetarian. When I was shipped over to Korea, I would trade the pork with someone else for bread."

Because of this, Howard did not feel that he had contaminated himself. So when he returned from the war, he resumed eating Kosher. This was to have a profound effect on his future family.

Yossie Willner was also drafted at that time. When Yossie was in the Talmud Torah, my father taught him many things that he should be careful to observe. "Why are you telling me, and not the other kids?" Yossie asked him.

My father answered, "I'm telling you because I know that you will keep it. The others will not. And if they know it is wrong, it will be a bigger Aveirah for them."

Shortly after Yossie arrived at Fort Dix, in New Jersey, to be inducted into the army, his name was called out, "Willner!" the Sergeant said.

I just got here, am I in trouble already? Yossie thought to himself.

"Report to the Captain's Office," the Sergeant said. The Captain told Yossie that a Rabbi Perr had called about him, and he was ready to help him in any way

From Fort Dix, Yossie was sent to Fort Jackson, in South Carolina. The same thing happened again. From Fort

Tzidkus Stands Forever

Jackson, he was sent to Camp Gordon, in Georgia. There too, this story was repeated. From Camp Gordon, he was sent to Fort Sam Houston, in Texas. There was no chaplain at that base, but shortly after his arrival, Yossie received a call from a chaplain, who was in a nearby airforce base.

"I'll never figure out how your father knew where I was going to go," Yossie said to me, "Even I didn't know where they were sending me!"

It was in a waiting room of Weill Cornell Hospital in New York that I met a bearded older gentleman. He introduced himself to me as Leimah Minkowitz. When I told him my name he reacted immediately with astonishment. "Rabbi Perr? I met a Rabbi Perr when I was a young child. It was in January 1953, we were refugees and we were put in a hotel in Manhattan, by the HIAS organization. Rabbi Perr came to the hotel and collected the children. He then took them down and registered them in Yeshiva Torah Vodaas."

Tzidkus Stands Forever

A few moments later, Rabbi Minkowitz added, "In those days, a Yeshiva would take in a Jewish child even without tuition."

I heard from someone who came here as a refugee child, a description of just how vulnerable the refugees were. They had lost everything. And in their concern and uncertainty about their futures, their children's chinuch was not the most important thing on their minds. Sending a child to Public School was the easiest option, and unfortunately it was chosen by many.

If I hadn't met Rabbi Minkowitz some thirty-five years after my father's passing, I would never have known this story.

It was in the early 1950s, and Philly Davidowitz was "Bar Mitzvahed" and long gone from the shul when, somehow, my father got his father Morris to start

Tzidkus Stands Forever

coming to shul regularly. Morris Davidowitz came to shul every Shabbos. He knew how to daven, and also became a gabbai.

When I say that Morris Davidowitz came to shul on Shabbos, it means, of course, that he walked. It also means that he came with empty pockets. My father always told people, "Do not come to shul if by doing so you will be mechalel Shabbos." If he saw someone in shul putting his glasses, or anything else, into his pocket, my father would gently and politely take it away from him, and then he would walk over to his house after Shabbos to return it personally.

Morris Davidowitz was not a storekeeper; he was a postal worker. Because of this, he was able to be in shul on Shabbos. Within a short time of his starting to come on Shabbos and learning with my father, he underwent a dramatic change in his commitment to Yiddishkeit. And then, one winter Friday evening, he didn't show up at all.

My father asked him, of course, where he had been, and Mr. Davidowitz answered, "It really is the fault of your Orthodox institutions, Rabbi." Mr. Davidowitz worked in the Williamsburg post office, and that Friday, the massive pre-Pesach mailings of Yeshiva Torah Vodaas and Bais Yaakov had come in. The postal workers were forced to work overtime sorting all the mail. Some of them had to say kaddish, so their supervisor, a Jew himself, gave them permission to stop work, and daven in the post office. They made a minyan and

Tzidkus Stands Forever

davened Kabbalas Shabbos and Maariv, and then they went back to work.

Mr. Davidowitz was quite proud of what his fellow workers had done, but my father was deeply upset by the story. On the way home he kept repeating to me and muttering to himself, "You hear, they were mekabel Shabbos and went back to work! These are Yidden who know how to daven. They were mekabel Shabbos! And what were they working on? The mail from Yeshiva Torah Vodaas and Bais Yaakov!"

This was the beginning of my father's campaign to stop Jews from mailing on Friday and Shabbos.

It was the Williamsburg post office where this incident occurred, but it wasn't only in Williamsburg where Jews worked in the post office. Throughout the whole New York area, there were Jews working in post offices. The postal service gave them secure employment, decent pay and good benefits. If a person didn't have money to start a business, or if someone didn't have a college degree, it was really a very good place to work.

It is true that my father was a person to whom it was hard to say "no." He was non-confrontational, ego-less, and truly a lishmah person. More important, he was a yorei shomayim. As the Gemara says, "He who possesses yiras shomayim, his words are heard." Nevertheless, Shabbos is the natural deadline of the Orthodox workweek. Things don't

Tzidkus Stands Forever

get done until they have to get done, and Friday is when they have to get done. Changing this habit in an institution is not an easy thing to accomplish.

However, my father did prevail on Yeshiva Torah Vodaas and on Bais Yaakov to stop mailing on Friday. I know that he also did the same with Mesivta Chaim Berlin. No doubt, he also tried to do the same with other Jewish organizations and individuals, but this was not just a simple matter of making a phone call and alerting these institutions to the problem. Usually there was at least some degree of resistance.

Of course, there were Rabbonim who took a stand that it was permitted to mail on Friday; and they printed their view on the subject in the Rabbinical Journal "Hamaor." My father worked on the sugya himself, and he was convinced that it was not permitted. I remember him spending an especially long time on the question of whether the mailman transgresses the Shabbos prohibitions for each individual letter in his mailbag. He also began to write an article on the subject. However, when he showed it to me, I suggested that he not publish it.

And so he did not complete it. I was afraid that his article, or any article, would not convince anyone. To this day, I'm not sure if my advice was correct.

On 4 Ki Savo 1956, Rav Aharon Kotler addressed a letter of support to my father, in which he wrote that

Tzidkus Stands Forever

sending mail on erev Shabbos or Yom Tov in places where Jews work in the post office is forbidden without question, and is a transgression of the issur of lifnei iveir. He also added that he had directed the Lakewood yeshiva office to not send mail on erev Shabbos or Yom Tov, and that there are also other important reasons not to mail on Friday, in addition to this issur.

Reb Aharon's letter is addressed simply, "To the honor of my friend Rav Menachem Perr." My father, in his typical self-effacing manner, had asked Reb Aharon not to write honorific titles in the salutation, so that he wouldn't be embarrassed to publish it and to show it to others.

On 25 Teves, 1956, my father received a letter on this subject from Rav Moshe Chevroni, Rosh Yeshiva of Yeshivas Chevron. Rav Chevroni also wrote that for many reasons it is forbidden to mail erev Shabbos. Rav Chevroni's letter was addressed, "To the honor of my dear friend; the precious one, of understanding heart." The letter closes with, "I remain, your friend and admirer, who respects you greatly, and who wishes you well, with great love. Moshe Chevroni."

According to the introduction to the article which my father was preparing to print in "Hamaor," he also had a third letter from another of the generation's great men. However, this letter has not been found.

I would guess that the writer of the third letter was probably Rav Yosef Eliyahu Henkin. Rav Henkin and my father

Tzidkus Stands Forever

were extremely close. My father discussed everything with him. They were in almost daily contact, and my father quoted Rav Henkin frequently. I doubt that my father would have undertaken this campaign without Rav Henkin agreeing with him, and Rav Henkin was not hesitant about taking a stand on anything he believed was right.

In every frum home before tissues became widely available, someone, usually a child, had the responsibility of preparing torn lengths of toilet paper for Shabbos. In the shul, I remember my father cutting rolls of toilet paper through to the cardboard tubes every Erev Shabbos, so that the daveners should not tear paper on Shabbos. I wonder how many other Rabbonim worried about such things in their shuls.

For several decades, there was a pharmacy on the southwest corner of Rockaway Boulevard and 131st Street, named Abrin Drugs. Oscar Abrin was a very fine person. He was our pharmacist.

Tzidkus Stands Forever

On an Erev Shabbos, my father entered the store taking my younger brother, Rav Eliezer, with him.

"Nu, Mr. Abrin," my father said, "when are you going to close your store for Shabbos already?"

"I've told you, Rabbi," Mr. Abrin answered, "I can't afford to close my business for Shabbos."

"So, at least take in a gentile to run the store on Shabbos," my father said.

"I can't do that, Rabbi," Mr. Abrin replied, "He'll steal me blind!"

"Well, at least don't smoke on Shabbos," my father said, getting to the point where he was probably heading in the beginning of the conversation.

"Rabbi, I swear," said Mr. Abrin raising up his hand, "I'll never smoke again on Shabbos!"

Sometime after my father passed away, I received a phone call. "Yechiel, this is Oscar Abrin. Do you remember me?"

"Of course, I remember you, Mr. Abrin!" I responded, "How are you?"

"Well, I'm retired now and I live in Florida," he said, "Yechiel, I'm ninety years old and I've decided to go to shul

Tzidkus Stands Forever

on *Yomim Noraim*. Could you get me a set of *machzorim*?" he asked.

"Of course, I will," I said, while thinking to myself, "aren't there any Judaica stores in Florida?"

"Let me take down your address." I answered.

"And Yechiel," Mr. Abrin interjected, "I want them with *Ivre Tiech*- the Yiddish translation."

Of course, Mr. Abrin might have decided to go to shul on *Yomim Noraim* anyway, but it is possible that it was his commitment to no longer smoke on Shabbos, all those years before, that finally brought him, in his old age, to seek after his roots.

Mr. Kaduk was a house painter in South Ozone Park. When my father tried to convince him to observe Shabbos, he explained that the people who hire him, want him to work on Saturday, because then they are home and can supervise his work. He finally did become a Shomer Shabbos. On one Shabbos he met me on Rockaway Boulevard, on the way to shul.

"I don't understand it," he said to me through a heavy stammer, "I didn't work on Shabbos for a year now, and I make the same money!"

Tzidkus Stands Forever

It was this concern for the shmiras Shabbos of others that led my father to his most well known innovation, the weekday Bar Mitzvah.

The Bar Mitzvah was the second most important family celebration in those days. The first was, of course, the wedding. In preparation for the Bar Mitzvah, every Jewish boy was sent for Bar Mitzvah lessons, even amongst non-observant Jews. There was a general misconception among non-observant Jews that Bar Mitzvah was connected in some way with becoming Jewish. They thought that it was the equivalent of "confirmation" by the Christians.

The Bar Mitzvah boy was resplendent in a new suit or, in the summertime, in a blue jacket with white "duck" pants. He was likely to wear his genuine hand-painted wide tie. The boy's hair was piled up in a pompadour, frozen in place with some kind of "gook," and crowned with a yarmulke, frequently made of blue and white panels. At some point during the celebration he would deliver his "Bar Mitzvah speech."

In the late 1950s, The Ponovizher Rov spent a Rosh Hashana with my parents in South Ozone Park. While there, he told my parents about a drosho he had given at an American Bar Mitzvah he had once attended. He said that at the end of the Bar Mitzvah speech, the boy raised both arms in the air and called down the blessings of Heaven upon his parents. The Rov was then invited to speak, and he said that when he saw the Bar Mitzvah boy standing just then with his

Tzidkus Stands Forever

arms up, he was reminded of the lawless times during the Russian revolution. At that time, it was common to see someone standing with his hands in the air while he was being robbed. And you could be sure, that if he was standing with his hands up, his pockets were empty. "And when I saw this boy standing here now with his hands up," the Rov said, "I became afraid that his pockets are also empty." The Rov's allusion to the tragic lack of Torah knowledge of these Bar Mitzvah boys was all too painfully obvious.

It was my mother who, with great relish, repeated the Ponovizher Rov's drosha to me. My father remained absolutely silent. Looking back, I understand that my father could not have been happy with such a drosho. It was not my father's way to be critical of the American Jews among whom he lived. At the same time, though, he wouldn't want to contradict the Ponovizher Rov; so he said nothing.

In those days every bar mitzvah boy received a "Bar Mitzvah set" comprised of a "silk" talis, actually it was rayon, with blue stripes, trimmed with "silk" fringes and tzitzis, and a shiny pair of tefillin, all in blue plush bags. My father saw to it that the talis was wide enough to be a minimal shiur. In addition, the tzitzis were removed and replaced with kosher woolen tzitzis. He did this also with all the taleisim in the shul. I helped him with this. And it is extraordinary that my father, who was not adept with his hands, would rapidly put in a perfect set of tzitizis, evenly tied, and evenly matched in length. He taught me how to do this as well.

Tzidkus Stands Forever

The tefillin in "Bar Mitzvah sets" were usually not kosher. My father was able to obtain tefillin with a hechsher from Israel. Then he would change the retzuos from what is called "Ashkenaz" to "S'fard." He told me that he did this because S'fard is easier to put on, since the tefillin can be held between the arm and the body while tightening the strap. He hoped that if their tefillin were easier to put on, perhaps the boys would actually put them on.

My father also changed his own tefillin to S'fard. He told me that the Chofetz Chaim had done so also in his old age. My father knew many things about the Chofetz Chaim. How he knew them, I do not know; but he did have a long friendship with Rav Mendel Zaks, son-in-law of the Chofetz Chaim. He may have been his source of information.

There was, however, a major problem with Bar Mitzvahs. The problem was that they were the cause of massive chilul Shabbos. The guests arrived in cars, and carried in the streets, and some even smoked in the vestibule of the shul.

My father was an amazingly innovative person who could come up with a fresh approach when he identified a problem. Using all his tenacity and influence, my father convinced the members of the shul that henceforth, Bar Mitzvahs would take place only on weekdays. He accomplished this despite the fact that some of the people weren't even sure that it was "permitted" to make a Bar Mitzvah on a day other than Shabbos.

Tzidkus Stands Forever

At first, the Bar Mitzvahs were made on legal holidays, when the families were free to come by car. It was a pleasure for them to be able to drive right up to the shul. Of course, the weekdays required putting on tefillin, but my father had a number of extra pairs of tefillin for those who didn't remember that tefillin were worn while davening. Later still, due to a shortage of legal holidays on the calendar, Bar Mitzvahs would be held on any day when the Torah was read.

My father made an effort to publicize the idea of weekday Bar Mitzvahs through articles and letters to various Jewish publications. In fact, in his generation of Rabbonim he became famous for having originated this novel idea. Yet at one point, after having started this campaign, he faced a deep personal decision.

Nathaniel Coller was a lawyer whose law offices occupied two adjoining store fronts on Rockaway Boulevard. He was a very fine and popular person; he had run for election for a judgeship and was a past president of the shul. And I remember when he stood up on the Bimah after Kol Nidrei to ask my father's forgiveness on behalf of the community.

Ten years before, as Mr. Coller told it, a man from Far Rockaway had brought his son to the Rabbi to be prepared for Bar Mitzvah. The Rabbi said to him, "There are fine shuls in Far Rockaway; why do you come here? Who is this boy's mother?'

Tzidkus Stands Forever

"The man answered, 'Rabbi, she is better than any Jewish woman.'

"The Rabbi said to him, 'I'm sure she is a fine person but she is not Jewish and your son is not Jewish. Making him a Bar Mitzvah is not what you should be doing. You should raise your son to be a good person until he is eighteen or twenty years old. Then, when he is able to make a mature decision, tell him, 'My son, I am Jewish; your mother is not. If you decide you wish to be Jewish you can study Judaism and become a Jew.' Then he will make a mature decision. But merely making him a Bar Mitzvah will be forcing him to be something he may not wish to be.'

Mr. Coller continued "The man went away to another shul nearby, and that Rabbi took the boy to the Mikvah and converted him, and made him a Bar Mitzvah. The people in our community had serious complaints against the Rabbi for turning away someone who wanted to become a Jew. The Rabbi was subjected to severe criticism.

"That was ten years ago. The boy is now 23 years old, and we have learned that he has just enrolled in a seminary to become a Catholic priest. Rabbi, it is the night of Yom Kippur, and on behalf of the community, I apologize to you and ask your forgiveness."

Besides being a fine person and a popular person, Nat Coller had also sustained a personal tragedy that had awakened the sympathy of the community for him.

Tzidkus Stands Forever

Nat Coller had had some problem with his back and a friend of his, who was a surgeon, told him that with a relatively minor surgical procedure, he could relieve his problem. He operated on him and paralyzed Nat Coller's legs.

The celebration of Bar Mitzvahs on weekdays only was already well established in the community, when Nat Coller told my father that he was planning to make his son's Bar Mitzvah on Shabbos, and that, of course, he would be coming by car.

My father had once said to me, "Yechiel, if you ever become a Rov, on the day you sign your contract you should write a letter of resignation and put it away in a drawer. Then you will be free to stand up for what's right."

I don't know whether my father had done this himself. But if he had not, it was only because he didn't need to. My father was prepared to leave the community over this issue. It was Reb Aharon's absolute opposition to my father's resigning, that brought about my father's reconsideration and eventual capitulation. And Reb Aharon was proven to be right. After that very painful Shabbos of the Bar Mitzvah, my father returned to the weekdays-only policy as if nothing had happened. There was never another Shabbos Bar Mitzvah in the shul. What I learned from this was that an exception can be made to a rule without losing the possibility of enforcing the rule. This was to be helpful to me years later in my work of running a Yeshiva.

Tzidkus Stands Forever

My father's efforts in this matter also brought about a number of weekday Bar Mitzvahs in other communities. Many years later, there still remained a great interest among Rabbonim in making weekday Bar Mitzvahs. Because there were a large number of inquiries from interested Rabbis, my parents drew up the following letter as a standard response. Of course it was my mother who composed the letter.

Dear

In reply to your inquiry Re: The week-day Bar-Mitzvah.

When we initiated the weekday Bar Mitvah in our Synagogue about 18 years ago, we began by utilizing all the civic and legal holidays when they occurred on Monday or Thursday, such as Labor Day, Thanksgiving, July 4th, Memorial Day, Washington's Birthday, etc., as well as those Sundays when there was "Krias HaTorah" on Rosh Chodesh, Chol Hamoed, Purim and Chanukah. These occasions presented no problem. The boy received an "Aliyah" and was honored by taking out the Sefer Torah and later returning it, accompanied by the singing of "Vayihi Binsoah" and L'David Mizmor respectively.

When the number of Bar Mitzvahs exceeded the aforementioned available days, we then found it necessary to make Bar Mitzvahs on civic and legal holidays when there was no "Krias Hatorah." Here I must say that we proceeded cautiously at first, not knowing what the reaction of the people would be.

Tzidkus Stands Forever

The boy was taught to "Daven" and to read the Haftorah of the preceding Shabbos. On the day of his Bar Mitzvah, he would conduct before the Omud either the entire daily services or as much of them as he was able. He would also read the Haftorah WITHOUT BRACHOS from a NOVI to show that he can read from a Sefer. However, we later found that the Haftorah was no longer necessary.

Today, we celebrate Bar Mitzvahs on any day of the week convenient to the celebrants. We usually arrange a late minyan. The services proceed slowly. The Bar Mitzvah boy conducts the services or part of them, wearing his tallis and tefillin. There is congregational participation and singing. If the boy wishes it, he also delivers a speech. Sometimes, if the parents insist upon it, we teach the boy the Haftorah, which he reads WITHOUT BROCHOS.

If the boy lives within walking distance from the shul, we encourage him to come to Shul the preceding Shabbos to be called up to the Torah, either with or without the presence of his parents. If he lives far from the shul, we arrange for his Sabbath stay, either at my home or with friends nearby. However, we do not consider this mandatory.

At the public services during the week, the family and friends gather from far and near. The atmosphere is a festive one and the pleasure and joy of the occasion is unrestricted. Since there is no violation of the Shabbos, everyone feels it is a real "Simcha Shel Mitzvah," for there is nothing to mar the celebration.

Tzidkus Stands Forever

From the pulpit, the Assembly is given to understand the reason for the week day Bar Mitzvah and the sanctity of the Shabbos is enhanced.

All those who have participated in and witnessed a week day bar mitzvah are convinced that a Bar Mitzvah is far more meaningful and beautiful when celebrated on a week day.

Menachem Perr

P.S. An "Aufruf" also results in "Chillul Shabbos" and should take place during the week. This too, can be done attractively.

This letter was not written on a letterhead, and it was not signed "Rabbi." My father understood full well the need for absolute purity of motive if one hopes to be blessed with Siyata Dishmaya to elevate the ruchnius of Yidden. Also, the term "without brochos" is emphasized throughout the text. To my father, nothing could be more wrong that trying to prevent desecration of the Shabbos while at the same time profaning the Divine Name by pronouncing Brochos when not permissible. Note also the spelling "brochos," in place of the more modern usage "brachot." My father had a past which he was not prepared to abandon. When my parents moved in their last years to Far Rockaway, my father

Tzidkus Stands Forever

asked me to get him a rubber stamp with his new address to use on his mail. I had a stamp made with the name Rabbi Menachem Perr.

He looked at it and said, "Why did you make it with 'Rabbi'? I don't like it to say 'Rabbi'."

"Why not?" I answered, "after all you are a Rabbi!"

"I don't want it, it's not necessary, Yechiel," he answered.

"Well," I said, "if you want, I could take a razor blade and cut off the 'Rabbi'."

"Good," he said, "do it!"

"But then," I said, "it will look funny, because your name won't be lined up with the address. Do you want me to make another one, or cut it off, or just leave it as is?" I asked. "Maybe you want to leave it for now, and then you'll see," I suggested.

And so it was left, temporarily, and it was never changed. It is interesting that my father as a young man had no difficulty with the title "Rav." On the personal stationary that he used when he was a Rov in Hartford, Connecticut, he printed in Hebrew "Horav Menachem Perr. Rav L'Adas Yeshurun. Merkaz Bais Yehuda, Rochester, NY. The expression Rav L'Adas Yeshurun conveys the sense of responsibility, and pride, which he took in his vocation.

Tzidkus Stands Forever

Although my father was rather shy throughout his life, he did not hesitate to take a strong stand as a Rov. But as he grew in greatness and in understanding, and he was one of those rare people who grew greater throughout his lifetime, he found the title "Rav" superfluous and also an encumbrance; and used it only when he was forced to.

I heard, from R' Chaim Bressler, that once at the table, my father said to my mother, "You should send Yechiel one or two pairs of woolen socks."

"Why?" my mother asked.

"Because my feet are cold," he answered. I was away, learning in Philadelphia at the time and because his feet were cold, he was worried about me.

Tzidkus Stands Forever

My father lost his mother, Chaya Sloveh in 1955. Sometime later, a thought occurred to me. "Dad" I said to my father, "that house in Coney Island belongs to you! You are the only son, and you are the *yoresh*; the heir!"

"Yechiel" my father answered, "My sister Chava lived with our mother and took care of her all these years. Let her have the house!" There was no further discussion.

My father wasn't a person who loved money. In fact, on occasion I heard him exclaim, "Money! I hate money! They do all the evils for money! People steal, and they cheat each other for money. Families are torn apart and won't talk with each other for the rest of their lives, and why? Over a few dollars of an inheritance."

When my father passed away, I recounted this in a eulogy at his funeral. A woman who was there was very inspired by this story. She was a daughter of a talmid *chacham*, and she was married to a businessman. She returned home, and hoping to inspire her teenage son, said to him, "Can you believe it? You know I just came from the funeral of a man who hated money!"

She had hoped to convey to her child some of the inspiration that she had experienced when she heard this. But instead, her son responded, "A man who hated money? What kind of a crazy man was that? How could anyone hate money?"

Tzidkus Stands Forever

The mother was terribly upset by her son's reaction. "What kind of a monster am I raising?" she said to my wife in anguish, and on the verge of tears.

Long before Pesach, my father began making preparations for the coming Yom Tov. My father was satisfied with machine shmurah matzos for his own use. He never used hand matzos, not because of any question of their kashrus, but simply because he was not interested in using them. For the sedorim he used the K'hal Adas Yereyim matzohs under the hechsher of Rav Yonoson Shteif. These were the matzohs which were preferred by the Litvish Roshei Yeshiva. For other matzohs, he used the Horowitz Margareten "18 minute" matzohs, which were under the hechsher of K'hal Adas Yeshurun. But his main concern before Pesach was to see that other yidden ate matzah on Pesach.

I remember one year in particular when he took me around with him; I was wheeling a baby carriage filled with cartons of matzohs. We delivered these cartons to many

Tzidkus Stands Forever

Jews who otherwise would not eat matzah. I remember one recipient who lived in a broken-down house and after much knocking finally came to the door. He was some kind of recluse and obviously had a strange personality. But he thanked us for the carton of matzohs.

I remember saying to my father, "But Dad, these people eat chametz on Pesach anyway!" He answered, "Yechiel, a person's stomach can only hold a certain amount. And where there is a kezayis of matzah, there is no room for a kezayis of chametz." Much later on I learned that Rav Yisroel Salanter had previously given this answer.

On Erev Pesach, he took care, of course, of the mechiras chometz to a gentile. My father always declined the usual gratuity which is given to a Rabbi for this service. In general, he never accepted any payments for his services. And when people insisted that he take a payment for sidur kidushin or the like, he would say that he was only taking it to give to a tzedaka, and then he would send the giver the receipt from the charity to show that he hadn't kept it himself. My father believed that taking money from individuals negated his influence on them for what was far more important: shmiras hamitzvos.

On a certain Erev Pesach, I was present at my father's mechiras chometz to a gentile whom he had used a number of times before. This Irish Catholic had a large family and lived in the first house around the corner from the shul. He often was hired to clean the shul and to do other odd jobs.

Tzidkus Stands Forever

This time, when he came for mechiras chometz, he brought along a young child who was acting out a bit. "Hey," he unexpectedly said to the child, "you should behave yourself here, after all you are one quarter Jewish!" My father, who had been explaining the process to him, fell silent for a while. Then he asked him how it was that his son was one quarter Jewish. "Oh, my wife's mother was Jewish!" the gentile answered. Before Yom Tov began my father delivered to their house five or ten pounds of matzah and some kosher l'pesach salami. I had long ceased to be astonished by his sense of achrayus, but this case astonished even me.

In the early afternoon on *Sukkos*, my father sent me around with a *lulav* and *esrog*, to visit a number of people who were unable to come to shul.

I remember taking the *lulav* to Mr. Walsky. Mr. Walsky in an apartment over a store. On the way there, a woman stopped me in the street.

Tzidkus Stands Forever

"I know what that is," she said, pointing to the *lulav*, "that is a siki." I corrected her, and continued on my way.

I found Mr. Walsky lying in bed. "Mr. Walsky," I said, "I've brought you a *lulav* and *esrog* to make a *brachah*." Mr. Walsky did not answer, but he slowly got out of bed, in his pajamas, and slowly put on a robe, and tied it with the sash.

Then, he walked to the sink in the other room, and washed his hands. He returned, and opened the little breakfront, and began slowly searching for his *machzor*.

"Mr. Walsky," I said, "Here, I have a siddur." I had brought the siddur along, tucked under my arm.

Mr. Walsky ignored me, and finally found his *machzor*. He slowly turned the pages until he found the *brachah*. He then turned to me, and took the *lulav* and *esrog* from me. He turned back, and began to say *"Leshem Yichud"*.

"Oh no," I groaned inwardly. Then, he began to cry. And then to sob. And then his body began to shake. He finally was able to control himself, finished the *brachah*, and handed back to me the *lulav* and *esrog*.

I had lost my impatience.

Tzidkus Stands Forever

My father's attitude towards American Jews showed itself in many ways. In particular, I remember a remark he once made.

There was a minyan for *shivah,* at the home of Emil Grasgreen. My father had brought with him several pairs of *Tefillin* for those who did not have any. I was helping some of the men put on the *Tefillin,* when Mr. Friedel came in. He was the owner of a large hardware store on Rockaway Boulevard, which was open on Shabbos, of course. Mr. Friedel picked up a pair of *Tefillin,* and expertly put them on, while reciting the *brachah* by heart.

On the way home, I told my father that I was surprised to see that Mr. Friedel must have once put on *Tefillin,* for a very long time. My father responded, "I'm surprised at you, Yechiel. Don't you know what this country has done to our people?"

My father loved this country. When my mother would do their taxes, my father insisted that she work it out in a way, where they would give at least a few dollars to the government.

But he loved *Klal Yisroel* more. And he laid the blame for their decline in religious observance not on themselves, but on the conditions they found in this country.

Tzidkus Stands Forever

Dorothy Willner grew up in a *Shomer Shabbos* family. She married Heshy Pearlman and eventually they moved to Holyoke, Massachusetts, where Heshy opened a bakeshop.

My father called Dorothy Pearlman every month to remind her to go to *Mikveh*. The *mikveh* was located in Hartford, Connecticut. It was an over-30 mile drive each way.

Rav Peretz Steinberg was very close with my father and was very often "drafted" by my father to get involved in some of my father's mitzvahs. On one occasion, Reb Peretz was "drafted" for a certain mitzvah in Jamaica, Queens; but as he and my father were passing a nursing home located on Hillside Avenue, my father suddenly said to him, "Reb Peretz, let's go in here for a minute." They went in, and my father asked for the administrator and introduced the two of them. "This is Rabbi Peretz Steinberg, and my name is Perr. We have come to you with a special request." Reb Peretz, who knew absolutely nothing of the special request stood there in stunned surprise as my father

Tzidkus Stands Forever

continued. "You know, the Passover holiday will be coming soon. We want to ask you to make matzohs available for your patients, so that they will not be forced to eat bread." Meanwhile, my father had taken a calendar from his pocket and was showing the administrator exactly when Pesach would fall out. The administrator agreed to make matzohs available, and my father went on to explain to him that the packages must be marked kosher for Passover.

The assurance of the administrator, however, was not the end of the matter. My father was ready with another suggestion. "You know," he told the gentleman, "if you break up matzohs in a bowl with warm milk and some sugar, it makes a delicious food. Your patients will love it much more than cereal!"

"Rabbi," the administrator answered, "We have a dietician here, and we are required by law to follow her directions. But if she agrees, we'll serve matzohs in warm milk." My father then thanked the administrator, and he and Rav Steinberg left the office.

They stepped out into the hall and Rav Steinberg turned to my father and said, "Come now, Rav Perr, this is just too much! Providing matzohs for goyim in a goyishe nursing home is also a mitzvah?"

"Oh," my father answered, "there are only goyim in this home? Come, Reb Peretz let us see, perhaps you are right."

Tzidkus Stands Forever

"What should I tell you," Rav Steinberg said to me, "We entered the first room off the hall, and went over to the first bed in the room, and the patient – I don't want to tell you his name – but his brother is the menahel of one of the largest Torah mosdos in New York."

It may be that my father knew what was going on in nursing homes because of Abraham Halpern. Mr. Halpern was a very eideler yid who originally owned a candy store on Rockaway Boulevard that was open on Shabbos. Mr. Halpern became very close with my father, and eventually he sold the candy store and opened a jewelry store across the street, which he closed on Shabbos. I remember my father working on the question for Mr. Halpern, of whether it is permissible to sell gold crosses for jewelry. Mr. Halpern's becoming shomer Shabbos, however, did not affect his children, and when he got sick, they placed him in a non-kosher facility. My father was very upset about this, but was unable to do anything about it. What he did do was to take packages of kosher food to Mr. Halpern several times a week. I don't know if it was the same facility that he later visited with Rav Steinberg, but I do know that he used to travel there by bus.

When my father was in his last years, he discovered that a nursing home, a kosher facility filled with Jewish patients, created problems for its patients on Yom Kippur. On Yom Kippur, just as on any other day, supper is served at five or six o'clock in the evening even though the fast is not over until much later. The elderly and frail patients, who are

Tzidkus Stands Forever

fasting, are faced with the choice of eating on Yom Kippur, or continuing their fast until breakfast the next day. When my father took this up with the owners of the nursing home, they said they could do nothing about it because serving supper was the responsibility of the day shift and not the night shift. So in the heart of one of the finest Orthodox communities in America, people who never ate on Yom Kippur were being forced to eat on Yom Kippur in their old age. My father's pain over this was intense.

A student of a former student of Rav Peretz Steinberg asked him a shailoh: is it permissible to act as an usher at a wedding performed by a Reform rabbi? "This is not a shyloh that you will find in the Shulchan Aruch," Reb Peretz answered, "but something else is very wrong here. How come they are getting married by a Reform rabbi? Are you sure that they are allowed to marry?" The young man made some inquiries and after a short time reported back to Reb Peretz that the bride had never been married before and there did not seem to be any problem with the wedding. "It can't be," Reb Peretz answered, "There

Tzidkus Stands Forever

must be something wrong! Why would they get married by a Reform rabbi? Keep checking!" The young man did as Reb Peretz instructed and shortly afterwards made a discovery. It was true that the bride had never been married before, but the groom had been married, and he had never given his first wife a get. Reb Peretz then contacted the groom, who told him that he would gladly give his first wife a get, but she wouldn't hear of it, and would not accept it.

At this point Reb Peretz made a call to my father. "Rav Perr," he said, "I've got a mitzvah for you." The two Rabbonim took the groom and went down to the East Side, where, under the guidance of Rav Moshe Feinstein, a get was written. The sofer was then appointed a shaliach to deliver the get to the woman. However, when the newly appointed shaliach heard that the woman lived in Hewlett, he backed out. "Ich fohr nisht kayn Hewlett – I'm not going to travel to Hewlett!" was his definitive response on the subject. Reb Peretz was then appointed as a shaliach instead, and he and my father went out to Hewlett.

Upon entering the woman's home in Hewlett, they met not only the lady herself, but also her fiancé, whom she was about to marry in a few weeks. He was a hulking goy who was about six foot four and built like a football player. A discussion followed during which the lady made it very clear to them that there was no way that she was going to accept any get from her first husband. The two Rabbonim left.

Tzidkus Stands Forever

However, as Reb Peretz says, "a mitzvah is a mitzvah" and one must not let problems get in the way. So the two Rabbonim returned to Hewlett three more times, each time finding no one home. On their third return, another goy started a conversation with them as they stood at the door of the house. "What do you want with her?" he asked. "You see that church?" He pointed towards a large structure at the corner. "Two, three times a week she goes there for lessons to become a Catholic." However, "a mitzvah is a mitzvah" and one mustn't be discouraged.

The two Rabbonim returned to Hewlett a fourth time, and this time they found the woman home. She still refused to accept the get, however this time Reb Peretz put the get down on her coffee table, saying to her, "This is your get!"

Reb Peretz says that he will always remember the smile of happiness on Reb Moshe's face when he told him what they had done. But the story didn't end with the get. My father had somehow found out that this woman had an aunt somewhere out on Long Island. He contacted the aunt and tried through her to prevent the woman from converting to Christianity. Whether he was successful with the aunt is not clear. But a few days before she was to convert, she had a fight with her fiancé and broke off with him, and that was also the end of the conversion.

It was during this period that my father began to pressure Reb Peretz to start writing Gittin. "The young generation will need Gittin," he told him, "and you are a

Tzidkus Stands Forever

young man." My father also got Rav Pam involved in convincing him. And finally Reb Peretz agreed.

"Oh, and one last thing," Reb Peretz told me as an afterthought, "when we were in this woman's house, your father managed to get a look into her refrigerator and he saw that it was pretty empty. 'Let's buy her some milk,' he said to me, 'so she shouldn't think that we're only interested in what concerns us.' And that's what we did. We went out and we brought her a couple of bottles of milk. That was typical of your father." My father never took upon himself the responsibility of writing a get, but he did take upon himself the responsibility to arrange a get when he knew of a divorce.

"Did you ever hear of a town called Shirley in New York?" Reb Peretz once asked me. I never had. "Neither did I," he admitted, "but your father took me and someone else out there with him to get some recluse who lived out there to give a get. How he found this person I'll never know. I only remember it taking hours and hours to find the place. This recluse lived in a wreck of a house out there, and your father got a get from him."

However, in at least one case my father's efforts came to naught. Among my father's papers, I came across a get that was written in the early 1940s and was never given. When I asked my father about this get, he told me that the woman had remarried long ago and refuses to accept the get. He tried to convince her from time to time but never succeeded.

Tzidkus Stands Forever

It was in my mid-teens before I realized that when I raised a question with my father, he would frequently respond, "Yechiel, what do you think?" This was very different from other experiences I had. I had a Rebbi in Yeshiva who warned the class not to write any questions or notes on the margin of our Gemaros. He explained that perhaps, someday a Talmid Chochom would happen to learn in our Gemaros and might waste his precious time trying to decipher the nonsense we wrote there. This was just one of the many ways in which we were told that we were just nobodies whose thoughts were worthless. I remember that one day I mentioned to my father the P'sak of a certain Posek. My father said to me, "And what do you think?" I answered, "Dad, what does it matter what I think. Who am I to have an opinion?" My father responded, "If you were wrong and they ask you in Shomayim, 'Why?' and you say that the Posek said it was muter, they will then ask you 'What did you think? You were old enough to have an opinion!' If you did wrong, what makes you so sure that you can blame it on someone else?"

Tzidkus Stands Forever

Years later I met an older man who is a great Yorei Shomayim and a great Ba'al Chesed. He told me that he had given my father a ride in his car and during their discussion my father had asked him, "And what do you think?" He was astonished by the question. He answered, "Rav Perr, who am I to think?" My father then said to him pretty much the same thing that he had said to me.

I once submitted an article to a certain Torah magazine. In it I mentioned a Hesped given by a certain Posek. I wrote that, "He put it well, I think." Shortly afterward I was called by someone on the editorial board. "If a Posek gave a Hesped who are you to think he put it well?" I didn't argue and agreed to delete the sentence. But I was taught differently by my father.

Tzidkus Stands Forever

It started as a casual conversation with someone who asked me how my father was feeling. That led to my finding out that my father had been severely beaten during a mugging. With my heart thumping, I raced my car down Rockaway Turnpike to South Ozone Park. When I saw my father, I couldn't look at him. His face was so severely swollen.

"Yechiel, why did you come? It's nothing, nothing," he said. At my prompting, he told me that he was coming home with a get late in the evening. It was a get that had taken him a lot of effort to arrange because the parties were not cooperative. But the get was finally written, and my father was the shaliach, and he was coming home with it in his pocket when someone stopped him and asked him for a light for his cigarette. My father had just answered that he didn't have a light, when he suddenly found himself lying on the ground while the mugger was going through his pockets. My father was wearing a denture, and from the blow to his face, he was cut on the inside of his cheek and was bleeding profusely. He was taken to the emergency room of Mary Immaculate Hospital. It required 13 stitches to close the wound. The mugger went through my father's pockets and found nothing of value. Then he found the get. As he unfolded it, my father, who was lying on the ground, said to him, "That is a religious document. It is of no value to you." The mugger looked at it and then threw it down and stalked away. "Fortunately," my father told me, "it only got blood on the back not on the writing. It was still kosher."

Tzidkus Stands Forever

"Was he a black guy?" I asked my father. "What difference does it make if he was black or white?" my father answered. He didn't like my question, and he refused to answer it. He was a totally unprejudiced person. To him, a person's worth had nothing to do with race.

I once had the opportunity to see how strongly my father felt about his responsibility to his community. In 1971 my wife and I bought our house in Far Rockaway. At the time we needed $10,000 for a down payment which we did not have. So I borrowed money from my aunts. When I asked my father's sister Chana Malka for a loan of $2,000 she said "I give it to you for a gift. Take it Tattele, for whom should I leave it?" Tante Chana had no children, and I was especially close with her. Nevertheless, in my mind I considered the money a loan. Gradually over the next few years we repaid all the loans, the last remaining was this $2,000, and in the interim Tante Chana had passed away. I thought through the matter, searched the halacha sources, and came to the conclusion that I did not have to return the money to her husband, my uncle Elya. Uncle Elya had been

Tzidkus Stands Forever

present and had been silent at the time of the original conversation, and therefore he had obviously agreed to the gift.

I discussed this with my father and he said "how can you decide such a thing for yourself. You are noge'ah bedovor?" I then asked a Rebbi in the Yeshiva to give me his opinion on the subject without telling him that it concerned me. The Rebbi also came to the conclusion that the money should not be returned. However when I reported this to my father he said "the Rebbi suspected that it concerned you even though you didn't tell him. He was prejudiced in your favor."

"Listen," I said to my father, "I'll just give the money to Elya and finished!"

"No, I'm not telling you to give the money to him," my father said, "I'm telling you that you have to know exactly what is the right thing to do!"

"I'll tell you what," I said to my father, "let's go and ask this shaila to Rav Yaakov Kaminetsky." My father liked the suggestion. He made a call to Reb Yaakov, and a day or so afterwards we were standing at Reb Yaakov's door on Saddle River Road in Monsey. The Rebbetzin greeted us warmly. "The Rosh Yeshiva wasn't feeling very well," she said to my father, "but when he heard that Rav Perr wanted to see him, he said there was no question Rav Perr must come!"

Tzidkus Stands Forever

Reb Yaakov and my father greeted each other with all the warmth of an ongoing friendship reaching back over sixty years. They exchanged some small talk. What I remember of it is Reb Yaakov reminding my father, with a smile, that he was the older of the two of them. We finally presented the question to Reb Yaakov. Reb Yaakov thought it over for a while and then said to my father, "your son is right. He should not return the money."

"And now I have another issue with my father," I said to Reb Yaakov. I then went on to tell him that my father had been mugged, and that the house had been broken into, and that we children were very anxious about the safety of both him and my mother. We wanted them to move out of South Ozone Park to a safer community.

Reb Yaakov sat up in his chair and questioned my father, "Nu Rav Perr, what do you say? Your children have a right to ask this of you!" I had raised this issue with my father a number of times before, and I was prepared to respond to the reasons he had given me for remaining in South Ozone Park. But this time he said something altogether new. "How do I know that I haven't been zoche to a long life because of the very fact that I remained in this place?" There was a profound silence in the room after my father said these words. Not another word was spoken on the subject. Not then or ever.

Tzidkus Stands Forever

I remember that I was driving my father somewhere when he suddenly asked me, "Tell me Yechiel, you are working to build a yeshiva; are you building it Lishmoh?" After a minute I said to him, "I've been thinking about it. What I think is that the Gemara says that if a person gives a Selah to Tzedakah so that his son should be well, he is a Tzadik Gamur. I think that I might have at least that much Lishmoh." My father remained silent and didn't say a word. I stole a glance at him and got the impression that he had an expression of satisfaction on his face. That impression carries me to this day.

A certain person who lived in Far Rockaway called the parents of a young woman who lived in another community and told them that their daughter's fiancé suffered from a serious illness. The engagement was broken, and many in the community were appalled by what the caller had done. Others, however, said that what the caller had done was tzidkus. I asked my father what he thought, and he immediately answered, "From this one incident you cannot tell if it was Tzidkus or Rishus. You can only judge by other things he had done. If he has done other acts of Tzidkus, then this is Tzidkus. If he has done other acts of Rishus, then this is Rishus."

Tzidkus Stands Forever

My brother, Rav Eliezer, repeated a conversation which took place at a Kiddush after Mussaf in my father's shul. It was 1973, after the Yom Kippur War, during the few months before Golda Meir was forced to resign as Prime Minister. Henry Kissinger was boasting that he was going to meet Golda Meir in Israel. Using "Shuttle Diplomacy," they would together bring peace to the Middle East. At the Kiddush, Mr. Abraham Halpern said to my father, "Rebbe, have you heard? Henry Kissinger is going to meet Golda Meir and they are going to bring peace to the Middle East."

"Mr. Halpern," my father said, and I'm sure he spoke in the tone that he used with me when I should have known better, "a man who could not make peace with his wife is going to meet with a woman who could not make peace with her husband, and they are going to bring peace to the Middle East? By us, we say 'Oseh Shalom Bimrovav Hu Yaaseh Shalom Aleinu' – 'He who makes peace in the heavens, He will make peace upon us also.'"

Tzidkus Stands Forever

In seeking to make contact with a certain individual, my father called a nephew who might be able to help. His nephew had a negative view of this individual and did not hesitate to express it to my father. My father hung up abruptly. A few minutes later, my father called his nephew and asked his forgiveness for causing him to speak Lashon Hora. This time my father would not hang up until the nephew would be mocheil him. When I was told the story many years later, the nephew was still careful not to mention the individual's name.

Around 1978, my father suffered a severe stroke. For a while he couldn't even speak, nor did he recognize his own children. Very slowly, he recuperated, and in about two years he regained all of his previous skills except for numbers. Numbers continued to plague him for the rest of his life. During his recuperation, he stayed for a while with my sister Rebbetzin Esther Tendler in Baltimore. There, he underwent an incident in which the sodium level in his blood dropped very low. He was hospitalized and put onto intravenous in Sinai Hospital. At the same time, Rav Yaakov

Tzidkus Stands Forever

Ruderman, the Rosh Yeshiva of Ner Yisroel, was also hospitalized in Sinai at the opposite end of the same floor. The Rosh Yeshiva always had a talmid with him to care for any need that might arise. On Erev Shabbos, Rav Ezra Neuberger was with the Rosh Yeshiva, and right before Shabbos, another talmid arrived to take his place for Shabbos. Knowing that my father was located at the other end of the floor, Reb Ezra decided to stop in and wish him a good Shabbos before leaving.

When Reb Ezra entered the room, he saw something unusual. My father's tefillin were lying unwound on the narrow table that goes over the patient's bed. Reb Ezra immediately thought that my father must be confused and doesn't realize that it will soon be Shabbos. Standing at the side of the bed he picked up one of the tefillin and began to wind it up. "Leave it! Leave it," my father said to him.

"But Rav Perr," Reb Ezra said, "it will soon be Shabbos and the tefillin should be put away." "You see" my father said to him "I am a choleh sh'ein bo sakono - sick but not in danger, and so I can ask a gentile nurse to do things that are chilul Shabbos, but not a yiddishe nurse. But how can I know if the nurse is a yiddish or not? So I left out my tefillin. And if a nurse comes in and says 'Oh, tefillin!" then I know she is yiddish. But if she says, 'What's this?' then I know she is not."

Tzidkus Stands Forever

It was after his stroke that we finally succeeded in moving him and my mother out of South Ozone Park. For half a year or so, they lived in my home. Finally they were established in their own apartment on Beach 9th Street, opposite the Young Israel. Very quickly, my father found that he had what to do even in Far Rockaway. In passing the shtiebel on my corner, he noticed that the z'manim board outside the shul said "candle lighting at sunset." He called the Rebbe's attention to the fact that candles must be kindled before sunset. Without another word, the Rebbe went out and removed the announcement from the board. Of course, it was the Rebbe who told me this, not my father.

On the front page of one of the Young Israel's publications was a photograph which contained a shem in very small print. My father pointed this out to the Rabbi for care in the future.

An appeal was made for baby clothing for poor families in Israel. My father enlisted Jack Brody, whose wife Zelda grew up in South Ozone Park, and Jack made it his own project, with much success.

A certain rabbi used to have the New York Times delivered on Shabbos, and it would lie on his lawn until Shabbos was over. My father said to him, "I'm not going to argue the halacha with you, but people will learn the wrong thing from you." The rabbi canceled his subscription. And of

Tzidkus Stands Forever

course, there must have been many other things that I don't know about.

As my father grew older, and his responsibilities grew ever more clear to him, he grew even more modest and self-effacing. In his very last years, after we were able to move him from South Ozone Park to Far Rockaway, he davened at the Yeshiva.

My father-in-law visited with us from time to time, and he always davened next to me "on the mizrach," at the front of the Bais Medrash. But my father chose instead to daven in the middle of the Bais Medrash, near the shulchan where the Torah is read. I wanted very much for him to daven in the front, but he demurred. "Dad," I said to him, "my father-in-law always sits on the mizrach; why won't you?"

"Yechiel," he answered, "in all my life I never sat on the mizrach, and I'm not going to do so now." Of course, this was something I had seen all my life. My father always davened as part of the Tzibbur, forgoing the traditional place

Tzidkus Stands Forever

of the Rov in shul in order to be next to the Baalei Batim. When he was near the congregants he was able to "show the place" to someone who couldn't or wouldn't follow along. He could inspire them to daven well by the example of his own Tefilos, which were always said loudly and carefully pronounced. Also, the fact that he was sitting nearby would restrain anyone who might have been tempted to talk during the davening.

But here in the Yeshiva, these reasons did not apply. Here, he could sit where it was appropriate for him to sit. I decided to give it one more try. "Dad," I said, "if you won't sit on the mizrach, people will say I'm a bad son. They will say I don't treat you with respect."

My father examined my face for a long moment, and then he shrugged his shoulders and said "Nu, nu," and turned away. The "nu nu" meant "so what."

On one previous occasion, I did succeed in getting my father to accept an honor. At the Bris Milah of my oldest son, Aharon Yosef, my father-in-law had been the Sandek. When Yisroel Moshe was born, I asked my father to be Sandek. My father said to me, "I'm surprised at you, Yechiel. Don't you know that you're supposed to choose an erlicher yid for a Sandek?" "Dad," I answered weakly, "some people say that you are an erlicher yid." "Nonsense!" my father answered, dismissing this possibility, and the possibility of his being a Sandek with a wave of his hand. "I know better!" Hoping to convince him, I said, "Dad, if you won't be the Sandek, there

Tzidkus Stands Forever

could be bad feelings in my wife's family over who should be the Sandek." This cast the question in different light, as I hoped it would. It was no longer a question of his honor alone.

My father withdrew into a thoughtful silence, and then he hesitatingly agreed.

That my father avoided the public eye doesn't mean that he had nothing to do with national organizations. To the contrary he was well aware of the activities of national organizations, and he did not hesitate to speak to their leaders when he had something to say about their activities.

Rav Dovid Lifshitz told me that my father frequently called him on matters in which the Agudas HaRabbonim was concerned. My father also tried to enlist the widest possible support in his campaigns against mailing on Erev Shabbos and for weekday Bar Mitzvahs. In addition, he was always an ombudsman for Chasodim for various individuals, and he also had many people for whom he needed Gittin, and whom he tried to prevent from transgressing the Torah. All these required frequent contact with the leaders and the influential people of his time.

In one case of which I know, a certain influential individual tried to avoid my father. I have no doubt that it was because he found it difficult to refuse my father's requests. I became aware that this person was avoiding my father when I once called his office, and his secretary came

Tzidkus Stands Forever

back on the line with the question "Which Rabbi Perr is this, please?"

Because of these many contacts, my father was well known and much respected by the influential people of his time. But my father's influence and the respect he received did not detract from his anava.

I remember what my father had said to me during, what I now realize, were the wonderful years when I learned privately with him. We were learning Chumash, and we came to where Moshe Rabeinu says to the Ribono Sh-l Olam that if He does not wish to forgive Am Yisroel, then He should erase Moshe from the Torah. At this point, I asked my father, since Moshe was the greatest anav in the world, how could he think that his name being in the Torah was important in any way?

My father answered me, "Tell me Yechiel, do you think an anav is a fool? Moshe Rabeinu knew very well who he was, and that there was no one else like him. An anav knows very well who he is, but it doesn't make a difference to him."

My father never spoke of what he had accomplished. He didn't keep score. I do know, however, that over the years he made a good number of Jews

Tzidkus Stands Forever

into Shomrei Shabbos. But even if someone would never become fully Shomer Shabbos, if he could be prevented from doing one melacha on Shabbos, or any other aveira, or one mitzvah, for my father it was worth the effort, and he felt required to try.

Shortly before my father passed away, he was taken to the local hospital in Far Rockaway with congestive heart failure. As he was being wheeled toward his room, he asked his cardiologist, Dr. Israel Brafman, for the name of the doctor who was with them and who would be on duty on Shabbos. Dr. Brafman, assuming that my father was concerned with the quality of the care he would receive over the weekend, told my father the name of the resident, and hastened to assure him that he was a competent professional.

But my father was not listening to Dr. Brafman's assurances. He had already started to tell the resident, who was leaning over his gurney, of the marvelously successful career of Dr. Rafael Moller. Both doctors must have been mystified by what must have seemed an irrelevant paean of praise for the success of some doctor in Washington Heights.

I didn't bother explaining to Dr. Brafman that my father's concern about who would be on duty was not at all about his own care. Although it was difficult for him to speak because his lungs were filled with fluid, he was laying the groundwork for explaining to the Jewish resident that one can be a successful doctor and also be Shomer Shabbos at

Tzidkus Stands Forever

the same time. My father was rarely in the hospital. He understood that if he was there now, he was in serious condition, but that was not his concern.

How my father came to know Dr. Moller, I do not know. But he seemed to have an uncanny ability to seek out and find tzadikim. In his last years, he used Dr. Moller as his physician. It was my privilege to drive my father to Dr. Moller's office, and the drive and the subsequent wait were well rewarded by the sight of these two elderly tzadikim greeting each other with great affection and deep respect. On one visit, Dr. Moller was upset with my father for not following his instructions. "Rav Perr," he said with the air of one bringing an irrefutable argument, "the Torah says 'ushmartem es nafshowseichem.'"

"Doctor," I intervened, "please do not tell my father what is says in the Torah. You know that it is he who decides what is said in the Torah!" Being himself a person who spent his own lifetime deciding what the Torah was demanding of him, Dr. Moller instantly recognized the truth of this remark. He and my father both glanced towards each other and their eyes met. They both recognized that they shared this same midah; and they both chuckled.

Throughout his life, my father had low blood pressure. In his last years, he had several bouts of congestive heart failure. On his last trip to the

Tzidkus Stands Forever

hospital, my father asked me to first drive him down to the water at the end of Beach Ninth Street. He sat in the car and looked at the ocean for a few minutes, and then he asked me to tell him the names of some of the places which can be seen from there. This was very unlike him. I had the feeling that having lived such an unworldly life, one might even say an anti world life, he wanted to take a look at the world. We sat a few minutes in the car looking at the ocean, and then he said, "Let us go, Yechiel," and I drove him to the hospital.

On that last stay in the hospital, I found out something else that I had always wondered about. My father had always had a badly swollen knee. It didn't show through his clothing, but I had seen it many times, and I asked him once about it. My father had answered me dismissively, "I got hurt," and I never asked again. This time in the hospital, the swelling opened, and fluid began to come out. The doctors inserted a plastic drain in the opening, and they asked me where the swelling came from. I sat down next to his bed and said, "The doctors want to know how you got the swelling on your knee."

"When I came home from Slabodka yeshiva," my father said, "my mother was afraid that I would be taken away to the army. So she took me to a doctor and he injected something into my knee and made it look like it does."

"Do you know what he injected?" I asked.

Tzidkus Stands Forever

"I have no idea," he answered. As he lay there in the hospital bed, the swelling gradually reduced until the knee looked perfectly normal for the first time since I knew him. I remember thinking to myself that if he had any flaws, this was a sign that his illness has cleansed them.

Early on the day before Yom Kippur, my father came to the Yeshiva. He wanted me to write out for him the amounts of food and drink permissible for the sick on Yom Kippur. Since he still had difficulty with numbers, he did not trust himself to remember the amounts, so he wanted me to write them out for him.

Later on that day, he would laboriously dial a list of about forty sick people, and he would explain to them how to eat these small amounts during the fast.

Kol Nidre and Maariv were uneventful. During Pseukei D'zimrah and Shacharis I kept looking at his place near the shulchan. His talis lay waiting for him on the table, but he had not come. I was a little apprehensive, but I had told him the day before that he should come late or even remain at home, because he was feeling weak and unwell.

During Krias HaTorah, I was told that there was someone who had to speak to me outside in the hall. I went out and was surprised that it was the Latino superintendent of my father's apartment house. A very nice fellow, he took

Tzidkus Stands Forever

my hand and led me into a classroom and then said, "I very sorry to tell you this thing, but your father he is dead."

"Are you sure?" I asked him in shock. "Yeah, I'm sure," he nodded his head sadly, "I'm sorry, so sorry."

As I walked towards my father's building, I saw an ambulance and police cars parked in the street. I stopped and asked a policeman, "Are you sure that nothing can be done, I mean resuscitation and things like that?"

"It's too late," the policeman said, and I could see the sympathy on his face.

My father had been found in the hall at the open door to his apartment. By the time I arrived, he had already been moved from where he was found into his bedroom. It seems that he had been davening Shacharis when he felt suddenly unwell. He had then gone out into the hall to seek help. He would never leave a sefer lying open, and even at this moment his old habits did not desert him. In his characteristic way, he had folded over a bunch of pages to mark his place and then closed the cover on them. When I opened the fold, I saw that he had been saying Nishmas. "The soul of all living will bless your name, O G-d our L-rd."

Tzidkus Stands Forever

My father's choice for his final resting place had been reported in one of the books by Rabbi Pesach Krohn. From there, it received worldwide retelling. It was even printed in German in October 1999 in Die Judishe Zeitung, Number 43, in Switzerland. I believe that it is his absolute giving of himself for an eternity, that touches and that moves so deeply.

What happened was that not long before he passed away, my father came to me in the Yeshiva and said, "I want to give you my tzava'ah. I wish to be buried in the shul cemetery. I want an ordinary matzeiva like all the others there, and with no shevachim written on it. The grave should be like all the others, and don't make a separation wall around it."

When I was able to speak again, I said to him, "But these are people who didn't observe Shabbos, and even among transgressors, we don't bury those of minor transgressions with those of major transgressions."

"I know, I know," my father answered, "but you know that the only thing that their children observe is visiting the cemetery. And when they see my matzeiva it will remind them of the things I asked them to do, to keep Shabbos, to keep kosher, and this will be a zechus for me."

"But haven't you reserved a place with the Rayim Ahuvim?" I asked. The Rayim Ahuvim was a group of

Tzidkus Stands Forever

distinguished Jews, many of whom were talmidei chachomim and tzadikim.

"I gave it up when I decided that my place should be here with the shul," my father answered.

"You gave it up; did you sell it back to them?" I asked weakly, knowing what his answer was going to be.

"Sell it back! Why should I sell it? I don't need it. Let them do with it whatever they want."

The moment that my father left me, I called Rav Moshe Feinstein. Reb Moshe answered the phone almost at once. "My father just told me that he wishes to be buried with his baalei batim, and they didn't observe Torah and mitzvos. Even transgressors are separated!" I said to him.

Reb Moshe heard how upset I was. "Vos iz! Vos iz!" Reb Moshe answered calmingly. "It is only a question of the honor of the deceased. If a person wants this, then doing what he wishes is honoring him!"

His resting place is marked by a simple stone with a simple inscription, as he had requested. We did allow ourselves to add the words, "Roeh Ne'eman Haya L'amo Ule'adoso" – "He was a faithful shepherd to his people and to his community." This addition was made on the basis of his once having said to my brother that if people would say about him that he was a faithful shepherd, it was something that he could accept as true. I also had asked Rav Yaakov Kamenetsky whether to add any additions to the inscription.

Tzidkus Stands Forever

Rav Yaakov did not want to tell me to do so against my father's wish, but he did say, "He must have forgotten that someday his grandchildren will come."

Although it is customary to inscribe only in Lashon Hakodesh on a monument, in keeping with his wish for continuing hashpa'ah on his community, we wrote his name in English.

It has been pointed out to me that his grave is listed on a website which lists the kevarim of tzadikim who have been buried in America. When I come to his kever, I often find more stones there than the family could have left.

When Rav Aaron Brafman called Rav Yaakov Kaminetzky the day after Yom Kippur to tell him that my father had passed away, Rav Yaakov exclaimed, "Oy! Who will now protect our generation?" And yet I do not doubt that my father was among those of whom it is said "tzidkaso omedes lo'ad" – "his righteousness stands forever."

And so surely he continues to protect!

Tzidkus Stands Forever

Mordechai Perkovitzky walking in the street of Drohichin. Note the shape of the cap, which was emblematic of Litvishe Yidden. In the picture on the right, he is speaking with Reb Meir Kaplan – Reb Meir was an uncle of Rav Avigdor Miller. The name Miller was changed from Kaplan.

Tzidkus Stands Forever

Reb Mordechai Perkovitzky at an older age and his wife Bobeh Henya. Her name was Appelbaum, and she was a cousin of the well known Mandelbaum Family whose house in Jerusalem gave its name to the Shaar Mandelbaum.

Tzidkus Stands Forever

Tzidkus Stands Forever

Front Row R-L: Chava Bluth, Zaida Reb Mordechai Zhaluzher, Bobeh Henya his wife, Bobeh Chaya Sloveh his daughter-in-law mother of the children, Fradel Lew.

Back row: my father and his sister Sarah Levine.

Missing: Reb Yechiel Yitzchok Perr and daughter Chana Malka who were in America.

Date of photo is probably around 1906-08. No doubt it was taken to send to my grandfather so far away from them in America.

Tzidkus Stands Forever

Reb Yechiel Yitzchok Perr. He shortened the name Perkovitzky and used the first name Ike.

Tzidkus Stands Forever

My grandparents sitting in front of their home in Coney Island, probably taken around 1920. Between them sits their nephew, Leibel Rosenbaum, newly arrived from Europe. Leibel eventually moved to Atlanta, Georgia and raised his family there. He and my father were very close, and he saved all the letters that my father wrote to him over the years. His Hebrew name was Yehuda Leib and he was probably named after Reb Leibke Perkovitzky, the grandfather we share.

Tzidkus Stands Forever

My father's mother, Chaya Sloveh, on the porch of her home in Coney Island. Her father was Reb Menachem Mendel. His family name was probably Kaminetsky. He was a learned man but died young. His wife was named Yehudis. She remarried and emigrated to Yerushalayim. She is buried on Har Hazeisim. Chaya Sloveh had an older sister, Malka. Malka had a son Dovid Kravitz, who lived in New York.

Tzidkus Stands Forever

My father as a young man. Although young men at that time wore no beards, many were careful to wear a mustache for *"Lo Yilbash."*

Tzidkus Stands Forever

The 1923 semicha class of Yeshiva Rabbi Yitzchok Elchonon. My father is third from the left in the back row. Third from the left in the front row is his future *mechutan,* Rav Isaak Tendler. Fifth from the right is the Maichiter Illuy.

Tzidkus Stands Forever

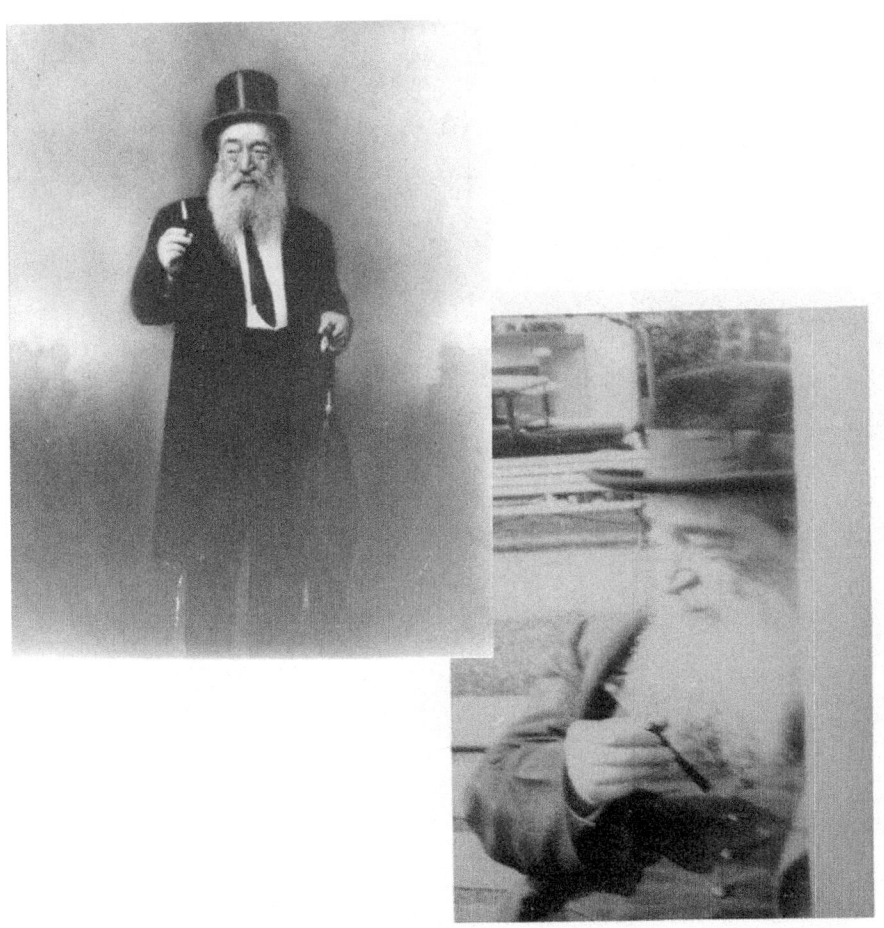

Rav Yosef Weinreb, my mother's father. He was the first Rav of Toronto.

Tzidkus Stands Forever

Rav Yoseph Weinreb, left, talks with his brother in law Shraga Feivel Kurtz. Reb Shraga Feivel was a Shochet and the grandfather of the Fruchthandler family. Photo taken at Allspectors Hotel, Jacksons Point Canada, around 1925, by William Turner.

Tzidkus Stands Forever

Matzeiva of Rav Yoseph Weinreb in the old cemetery of Toronto, Canada. Note the wall around the grave. My father specified that he did not want this done to his grave

Tzidkus Stands Forever

Congregation Sons of Israel 127-05 Foch Boulevard, South Ozone Park, New York. My father was deeply concerned that this building should never be sold so that it not be used for a church. It stood empty until vandals set it aflame and it was completely destroyed. The flag pole on the right was a gift from the Veterans of Foreign wars, whose post was next door to the left of the shul, and whose admiration for my father was shared by many of the gentiles in the neighborhood.

Tzidkus Stands Forever

Photo of my parents, taken in the dining room of their home 116-30 130th Street, South Ozone Park. On the right is a staircase going up. To the left is the bookcase on the top of which the Sefer Torah lay for more than ten years.

Tzidkus Stands Forever

The front of what had once been an Orthodox Shul on Sutphin Boulevard, as it appears today (2011), about 60 years after we removed the Torah. Note the Cupola still standing on the roof. The window to the left served as our access. At that time, there were no bars on it.

Tzidkus Stands Forever

Semicha from Yeshiva Rav Yitzchok Elchonon. The *Maichiter Iluy* is signed on the top line to the left.

בעז'ה'ית
הרב החריף ובקי
ר' מנחם מענדל בכ"ר יחיאל יצחק פער
גמר חוק למודו בישיבת רבנו
יצחק אלחנן ז"ל יגע ומצא כדי מדתו
בתורה ובחכמה וסמכנו אותו בסמיכת
חכמים יורה יורה ובשפ"ר רב יתקרי להורות
באו"ה ולנהל עדתו על דרכי התורה והיראה
ולירא' באנו על החתום יום ו' עש"ק כ"א
לחדש אדר שנת התרפ"ג לפ"ג

נאום ... נאום
נאום ... נאום
נאום

Tzidkus Stands Forever

Semicha from Rav Issac Sher, Rosh Yehiva of Slabodka Yeshiva

בְּעֶזְרַת הַשֵׁם

קוּשְׁטְ אמרי אמת נתן להאמר להודיע שבחו של האי גברא רבא ויקירא הוא ניהו כבוד ידידי הרב הג' עדיו לגאון בישראל כש"ת מוהר"ר מנחם מענדיל פערר נ"י הוא מיקירי תלמידי ישיבתנו כנסת ישראל בסלבודקה שעלה והצליח בהצלחת התורה להיות מורה הוראה בישראל. וכבר סמכוהו רבנן ונתנו לו הורמנא דמלכא. ואני מצטרף עמהם לֵאמֹר

יוֹרֶה יוֹרֶה יָדִין יָדִין כְּאַחַד הַמוֹרִים הַמֻבְהָקִים בְּיִשְׂרָאֵל

ידידי הגדול הוא מפורסם לתהלה בשערים המצוינים בהלכה בבקיאות גדולה בש"ס ראשונים ואחרונים וחריפות עצומה לחדש חדושים עמוקים ומתוקים בשכל זך וישר בכל מקצועות שבתלמוד ופוסקים לאסוקי שמעתתא אליבא דהלכתא ומלבד גדלו בתורה הוא גדול בדעת ויר"ש טוב וישר במעלות המדות רצוי ונעים בכל הנהגותיו. השפעתיו רבה ע"י דרשותיו המלאות ענין בעומקה המחשבה בצירוף בצירוף נועם אמרי פה כופיק מרגליות :

אשרי העיר שעתהדר בו לשום עטרת הרבנות על ראשו כי ילמו לאורן ויתבסמו מתורתו ברב אושר והצלחה כמאמרם ז"ל תיקף

לתה"ח ברכה כתבתי וחתמתי לכבוד התורה וגדוליה :

ט"ו לחדש תמוז תרפ"ה פה ניו יורק :

Tzidkus Stands Forever

Semicha from Rav Aharon Kotler

Tzidkus Stands Forever

Cover letter sent by Rav Aharon Kotler to my father together with the original letter that he received from France.

Behrend Strauss born Hamburg
10. VI. 1913

Address: Strauss
Castelferrus Tarn et Garoone

Tzidkus Stands Forever

Letter given to my father about mailing Erev Shabbos.

My father asked Rav Kotler not to write any honorifics in the greeting so that he wouldn't be embarrassed to show it to others

בית מדרש גבוה באמריקה
BETH-MEDRASH GOVOHA OF AMERICA
Rabbi Aaron Kotler　　　　　אהרן קאטלער
617 SIXTH STREET, LAKEWOOD, N.J.

ב"ה ד' תבוא שנת תשט"ו

כבוד ידידי הרב מוה"ר מנחם פערר שליט"א

אחד"ש בידידות,

נדון שאלתו אם מותר לשלוח מכתבים ומשלחינו ע"י הדואר בעש"ק או בערב יום טוב במקומות שמוזרים לוב עובדינו יהודים בהדואר ובאים עי"ז לידי חלול שבת, הצבר מזוט לאסור ועוברים בלאו דלפני עור, וי"ש לבאר הדבר באורפה ו ין כאן מקום, כף ההלכה ברורה פו"

/וב"ה הנהגתי כן בלשכת דישיבתנו שלא לשלוח בעש"ק ובערב יו"ט/ וישנן עוד פעמים חשובים למנוע מזה, ואמר שלו" וברכת כט"ס לכה"ר
מוקירו ומכבדו /אהרן קטלר

Tzidkus Stands Forever

Tzidkus Stands Forever

AFTERWORD

It was about a year ago (2016), that I was searching for something among some old papers, when I came across a note that I had put aside several years before. The note was on a letterhead and it had come to the Yeshiva with a donation. I was sure that the donation had been receipted properly, but that I had put aside the note in order to write a personal response also.

The three line letterhead read "Long Island University. College of Pharmacology. Professor Edgar Schwartz."

Of course I remembered Edgar very well. I would sit on the steps of my father's shul and watch Edgar and his kid brother, Howie, playing fierce games of handball against the wall of the American Legion building, next door.

I had no idea if I could still reach Edgar, but I dialed the first of the phone numbers listed on the letterhead.

"Professor Schwartz," A man answered.

"Professor Schwartz," I said, "This is Yechiel Perr."

A long silence.

And then, "Oh my gosh!" And a long conversation ensued.

Tzidkus Stands Forever

Among the many things that Edgar said to me was, "we all know that the future of Yiddishkeit belongs to the Frum. But what can we do? They are so insular that we cannot get close to them!"

He also told me that he and Howie walk to daven, they never ride. This he explained was my father's influence.

I mentioned that I had written a short biography of my father.

"I know. I read it," he said to my surprise.

"But it was not distributed widely. How did you happen to read it?" I asked.

"Well," he said, "Howie has two observant daughters, and each was shopping for a Father's Day gift for him in a Judaica store. They both happened to buy him the same book. So since he had two, he gave one to me."

"But how did they know to buy this book?" I asked.

"Oh," he answered, "Rabbi Perr is a household name by us. We mention him all the time."

After the call ended, I immediately called my brother.

"Eliezer," I said, "Can you believe it? Howie Schwartz has two Frum daughters!"

Tzidkus Stands Forever

"And you haven't called him?" my brother asked, "That's not like you! Come on! Call him up!"

I felt uncomfortable about calling Edgar for Howie's number, so I found the number for Howard Schwartz in the phone book, and I made the call. No one answered.

Lunch time, I went home from the Yeshiva and called again. Again, no answer.

Supper time, I called again, and a woman answered.

"Mrs. Schwartz," I asked her, "May I ask you if you have a brother-in-law named Edgar Schwartz?"

"Yes, of course," she said. "That's my husband's brother."

"Mrs. Schwartz," I said, "This is Yechiel Perr."

"Rabbi Yechiel Perr!" She exclaimed. "I don't believe it! How are you?"

"Thank G-d," I responded.

"Thank G-d?" she corrected me, "Baruch Hashem!" She said emphatically. "Do you know where I was today, Rabbi?" She asked me.

"No, I don't. But I tried you a few times, and I know you weren't home."

Tzidkus Stands Forever

"I was in Passaic," she said, "at my eight-year-old grandson's Chumash party in his Yeshiva! Oh," she said, "Your father would be so proud of us!"

"May I ask you," I questioned hesitantly, "How did you come to be frum?"

"Well," she said, "Your father had a profound influence on the boys, and they decided that they would only have Kosher homes. When they dated my sister-in-law and myself, they told us that we must keep Kosher.

"Once we were keeping Kosher, we decided to send our girls to the Hillcrest Jewish Center afternoon school. The girls became attracted to religion, and they became religious!"

A few months later, my wife and I attended the Partners in Torah weekend of our good friends, Rabbi Eli and Chanie Gewirtz.

After Mincha, a young man approached me whom I didn't know. He looked like some young man who learned in a Kollel.

"Rabbi Perr?" He asked.

"Yes."

"My name is Hillel Isseroff," he said. "I am the son-in-law of Howard Schwartz. My wife is here, and she would love to meet you. Is this possible?"

Tzidkus Stands Forever

"Of course it is. I would love to meet her! You see those tables in the corner of the Dining Room? My wife and I made up to meet there for Shalosh Seudos. Perhaps we can meet with your wife over there."

My wife and I had just made Hamotzi when Shoshana Isseroff came over to meet us, with her eight children. The youngest was in a stroller, and then all the way up, toddlers to pre-teens. All the boys with short haircuts, and all the girls in skirts. All of them staring at me wordlessly.

"I owe this all to your father," the proud mother said to me.

And Shoshanna Isseroff herself, what can I say, she has a glow on her face that says, "I am a fulfilled person!" A face filled with happiness and contentment.

Interestingly, although Dr. Hillel Isseroff has his medical practice in Brooklyn, his home is in Passaic, a few houses away from my sister's daughter, my niece Brochah Skulnick. They are very close friends. And they never knew of the connection.

Tzidkus Stands Forever

Introduction	7
Drohitchin	11
Yeshiva	14
R' Aharon and R' Yaakov	21
America	27
Coney Island	34
Rabbanus	38
Marriage	43
1930's	46
South Ozone Park	48
Talmud Torah	53
Intermarriage	58
R' Aharon in America	61
Two Incidents	65
Hatzalah	66
R' Sender Vigodsky	69
Pearl Harbour	72
Shul	75
"Nisht kosher!"	81
Lost and Found	86
Memorial Day	91
The Neighbor	94
Eliyahu Hanavi	95
"I am the Rabbi,"	99
Sefer Torah	101
Korean War	110
Shabbos	113
Bar Mitzva	121
"I Hate Money!"	132
Pesach	133
Sukkos	135
R' Peretz Steinberg	138
"What do you think?"	145
Din Torah	148
Anivus	156
Petirah	162

Made in the USA
Middletown, DE
29 November 2020